The Air Fryer
Meal Prep
Cookbook

2000 Days of Health-Conscious and Nutrient-Rich Recipes with a
4-Week Step By Step Meal Prep to Hone Your Culinary Adventure

Jacqueline R. Izaguirre

Editor: AALIYAH LYONS

Interior Design: BROOKE WHITE

Cover Art: DANIELLE REES

Food stylist: Sienna Adams

Table Of Contents

Introduction

In the realm of culinary innovation, one kitchen appliance has truly taken the culinary world by storm, revolutionizing the way we prepare our favorite dishes and significantly transforming our relationship with food. The air fryer, a compact and versatile kitchen wonder, has become an indispensable tool for home chefs seeking a healthier, more convenient, and incredibly delicious way to enjoy their favorite meals. with its remarkable ability to cook and crisp with less oil, it has brought the concept of guilt-free indulgence to the forefront of cooking, providing us with a powerful ally in our quest for a balanced lifestyle.

The Air Fryer Meal Prep Cookbook is your comprehensive guide to harnessing the full potential of this culinary marvel. In the pages that follow, you will embark on a culinary journey that offers a perfect fusion of modern innovation and the timeless art of meal preparation. with a primary focus on air frying, the cookbook is designed to enhance your cooking experience, making it more convenient, healthier, and remarkably delicious.

Embracing the Air Fryer Revolution

For those of you who are new to the concept of air frying, let me introduce you to this transformative kitchen companion. An air fryer is a countertop appliance that uses hot air to cook and crisp food, much like a deep fryer, but with far less oil. It's a healthier alternative to traditional frying methods, as it significantly reduces the fat content in your favorite dishes, yet still delivers that mouthwatering, crispy texture we all love. with the Air Fryer Meal Prep Cookbook as your guide, you'll quickly learn that this appliance is much more than just a "fryer"; it's a multifunctional kitchen workhorse that can bake, roast, grill, and even dehydrate.

In this cookbook, we'll dive deep into the world of air frying and explore its incredible versatility. You'll be amazed at how it can simplify your meal preparation, save you time, and allow you to enjoy your favorite dishes with a fraction of the calories you'd typically consume. From classic comfort foods to exotic international cuisine, the air fryer empowers you to recreate a wide array of dishes in a healthier and more convenient manner.

Mastering the Art of Air Frying

The magic of an air fryer lies in its ingenious cooking process, which allows you to achieve the crispy, golden results of deep frying with significantly less oil. Here's how it works:

- Rapid Hot Air Circulation: The air fryer is equipped with a heating element and a powerful fan. When you set the desired temperature, the heating element quickly warms the air inside the cooking chamber. The fan then circulates this hot air at a high speed, ensuring even heat distribution throughout the cooking process.
- Convection Cooking: This method is known as convection cooking. It's different from traditional frying, where food is submerged in hot oil. In the air fryer, hot air is used to cook the food, and this process creates a similar, crispy texture on the outside while maintaining the tenderness inside.
- Minimal Oil: While a small amount of oil can be used to enhance flavor and crispiness, it's a mere fraction of what you'd need for deep frying. Most air-fried dishes require just a light spritz of oil or none at all, making it a much healthier alternative.
- Versatile Cooking: Air fryers are incredibly versatile, capable of baking, roasting, grilling, and even dehydrating in addition to air frying. This means you can cook a wide variety of dishes and achieve different textures, all in one compact appliance.

How to Use This Book

The Air Fryer Meal Prep Cookbook is designed to cater to both newcomers to air frying and seasoned air fryer enthusiasts. No matter your skill level, this book will equip you with the knowledge, inspiration, and practical recipes you need to master the art of air frying and meal prepping.

Beginners' Guide

If you're new to air frying, the beginning chapters of this book are tailored just for you. You'll find a comprehensive introduction to your air fryer, explaining how it works, what to look for when buying one, and essential tips for getting started. We'll also provide guidance on how to properly care for your air fryer, ensuring it remains a reliable kitchen companion for years to come.

Meal Prep Made Easy

In today's fast-paced world, the concept of meal prepping has gained immense popularity. It's a life-changing practice that not only saves you time and money but also encourages healthier eating habits. This cookbook combines the power of air frying with the convenience of meal prep, helping you streamline your cooking process and allowing you to maintain a nutritious diet with ease.

The book contains a meticulously curated four-week meal prep plan, designed to simplify your weekly food preparation routine. Each week is thoughtfully structured with breakfast, lunch, and dinner recipes, making it easier than ever to achieve your dietary and fitness goals. Whether you're looking to lose weight, save time, or simply enjoy delicious, homemade meals on a busy schedule, this meal prep plan has got you covered.

Our meal prep approach is not about dull, repetitive meals; it's about creativity, variety, and, most importantly, enjoying the food you eat. We've included a wide array of recipes that cater to diverse tastes and dietary preferences. Whether you're a meat lover, a vegetarian, or follow a specific diet, there's something for everyone. Expect to explore a rich collection of flavors, ingredients, and cuisines from around the world, all prepared in the versatile air fryer.

Navigating the Cookbook

This cookbook is thoughtfully organized to make your culinary adventure straightforward and enjoyable. Each recipe is accompanied by clear, step-by-step instructions, ingredient lists, and nutritional information.

You'll find recipes for appetizers, main courses, sides, and even delightful desserts that can be effortlessly prepared in your air fryer. We've taken special care to include a wide array of recipes suitable for different dietary needs, so whether you're following a low-carb, keto, paleo, or vegetarian diet, you'll find recipes that meet your preferences.

To make meal prep even simpler, the cookbook includes shopping lists and weekly meal plans that lay out each day's meals and snacks. These plans are designed to help you stay on track with your goals while saving time and effort in the kitchen.

As you embark on your culinary journey with *The Air Fryer Meal Prep Cookbook*, remember that the power of the air fryer lies not only in its ability to create healthier versions of your favorite dishes but also in its capacity to make your life easier. Meal prepping with the air fryer is a dynamic duo that ensures you spend less time in the kitchen and more time savoring the delicious results.

with this cookbook as your companion, you'll discover that meal prepping can be an enjoyable, rewarding experience, helping you maintain your health and balance without sacrificing flavor or variety. You'll be amazed at the vibrant, wholesome meals you can prepare in your air fryer, and how convenient and cost-effective this practice can be.

Welcome to the world of air frying, meal prepping, and a healthier, more delicious way of enjoying the food you love. It's time to roll up your sleeves, fire up your air fryer, and embark on a journey that will transform the way you cook and eat. We hope *The Air Fryer Meal Prep Cookbook* will inspire you, simplify your kitchen routine, and leave you craving every meal you prepare.

Bon appétit and happy air frying!

Air Fryer Cooking Chart

Beef					
Item	Temp (°F)	Time (mins)	Item	Temp (°F)	Time (mins)
Beef Eye Round Roast (4 lbs.)	400 °F	45 to 55	Meatballs (1-inch)	370 °F	7
Burger Patty (4 oz.)	370 °F	16 to 20	Meatballs (3-inch)	380 °F	10
Filet Mignon (8 oz.)	400 °F	18	Ribeye, bone-in (1-inch, 8 oz)	400 °F	10 to 15
Flank Steak (1.5 lbs.)	400 °F	12	Sirloin steaks (1-inch, 12 oz)	400 °F	9 to 14
Flank Steak (2 lbs.)	400 °F	20 to 28			

Chicken					
Item	Temp (°F)	Time (mins)	Item	Temp (°F)	Time (mins)
Breasts, bone in (1 1/4 lb.)	370 °F	25	Legs, bone-in lb.)	380 °F	30
Breasts, boneless (4 oz)	380 °F	12	Thighs, boneless (1 1/2 lb.)	380 °F	18 to 20
Drumsticks (2 1/2 lb.)	370 °F	20	Wings (2 lb.)	400 °F	12
Game Hen (halved 2 lb.)	390 °F	20	Whole Chicken	360 °F	75
Thighs, bone-in (2 lb.)	380 °F	22	Tenders	360 °F	8 to 10

Pork & Lamb					
Item	Temp (°F)	Time (mins)	Item	Temp (°F)	Time (mins)
Bacon (regular)	400 °F	5 to 7	Pork Tenderloin	370 °F	15
Bacon (thick cut)	400 °F	6 to 10	Sausages	380 °F	15
Pork Loin (2 lb.)	360 °F	55	Lamb Loin Chops (1-inch thick)	400 °F	8 to 12
Pork Chops, bone in (1-inch, 6.5 oz)	400 °F	12	Rack of Lamb (1.5 - lb.)	380 °F	22
Flank Steak (2 lbs.)	400 °F	20 to 28			

Fish & Seafood					
Item	Temp (°F)	Time (mins)	Item	Temp (°F)	Time (mins)
Calamari (8 oz)	400 °F	4	Tuna Steak	400 °F	7 to 10
Fish Fillet (1-inch, 8 oz)	400 °F	10	Scallops	400 °F	5 to 7
Salmon, fillet (6 oz)	380 °F	12	Shrimp	400 °F	5
Swordfish steak	400 °F	10	Sirloin steaks (1-inch, 12 oz)	400 °F	9 to 14
Flank Steak (2 lbs.)	400 °F	20 to 28			

Vegetables					
INGREDIENT	**AMOUNT**	**PREPARATION**	**OIL**	**TEMP**	**COOK TIME**
Asparagus	2 bunches	Cut in half, trim stems	2 Tbsp	420°F	12-15 mins
Beets	1 1/2 lbs	Peel, cut in 1/2-inch cubes	1 Tbsp	390°F	28-30 mins
Bell peppers (for roasting)	4 peppers	Cut in quarters, remove seeds	1 Tbsp	400°F	15-20 mins
Broccoli	1 large head	Cut in 1-2-inch florets	1 Tbsp	400°F	15-20 mins
Brussels sprouts	1 lb	Cut in half, re-move stems	1 Tbsp	425°F	15-20 mins
Carrots	1 lb	Peel, cut in 1/4-inch rounds	1 Tbsp	425°F	10-15 mins
Cauliflower	1 head	Cut in 1-2-inch florets	2 Tbsp	400°F	20-22 mins
Corn on the cob	7 ears	Whole ears, remove husks	1 Tbps	400°F	14-17 mins
Green beans	1 bag (12 oz)	Trim	1 Tbps	420°F	18-20 mins
Kale (for chips)	4 OZ	Tear into pieces, remove stems	None	325°F	5-8 mins
Mushrooms	16 OZ	Rinse, slice thinly	1 Tbps	390°F	25-30 mins
Potatoes, russet	1 1/2 lbs	Cut in 1-inch wedges	1 Tbps	390°F	25-30 mins
Potatoes, russet	1 lb	Hand-cut fries, soak 30 mins in cold water, then pat dry	1/2 -3 Tbps	400°F	25-28 mins
Potatoes, sweet	1 lb	Hand-cut fries, soak 30 mins in cold water, then pat dry	1 Tbps	400°F	25-28 mins
Zucchini	1 lb	Cut in eighths lengthwise, then cut in half	1 Tbps	400°F	15-20 mins

Chapter 1

Step-By-Step Meal Plans

Meal Plan Week 1

BACON AND EGG SANDWICHES

Prep time: 10 minutes | Cook time: 12 minutes | Serves 4

How to serve: Serve two tofu eggs and one piece of vegan bacon on each biscuit.
How to store: Refrigerate any leftover sandwiches in an airtight container for up to 2 days.

TACO WRAPS

Prep time: 5 minutes | Cook Time: 25 minutes | Serves 4

How to serve: Fill the tortillas with the nuggets and vegetables, fold them up, and serve immediately, garnished with mixed greens.
How to store: Store any uneaten taco wraps in the refrigerator for up to 2 days. Keep the components separate for the best texture.

ZUCCHINI PARMESAN CHIPS

Prep time: 20 minutes | Cook time: 15 minutes | Serves 10

How to serve: Sprinkle with salt and serve with salsa.
How to store: Store any leftover chips in an airtight container at room temperature for up to 2 days. Reheating in the air fryer can help restore their crispiness.

AIR-FRIED SPINACH FRITTATA

Prep time: 5 minutes | Cook time: 10 minutes | Serves 4

How to serve: Slice and serve warm.
How to store: Refrigerate any remaining frittata in an airtight container for up to 3 days. Reheat gently in the air fryer or microwave.

ZUCCHINI TURKEY BURGERS

Prep time: 10 minutes | Cook time: 10 minutes | Serves 5

How to serve: Place in buns with ketchup and lettuce and enjoy.
How to store: Store any leftover turkey burgers in the refrigerator for up to 2 days. Reheat in the air fryer or oven for best results.

BETTY'S BEEF ROAST

Prep time: 5 minutes | Cook Time: 60 minutes | Serves 6

How to serve: Serve the beef roast when it's done cooking.
How to store: Store any leftover beef roast in the refrigerator in an airtight container for up to 3 days. Reheat slices in the air fryer or microwave.

PARMESAN & GARLIC CAULIFLOWER

Prep time: 5 minutes | Cook Time: 40 minutes | Serves 4

How to serve: Serve the cauliflower when it's golden brown.
How to store: Store any leftover cauliflower in the refrigerator in an airtight container for up to 3 days. Reheat in the air fryer or oven to maintain its crunch.

WEEK 1 SHOPPING LIST

PANTRY:

- Nutritional yeast (1/4 cup plus 2 tablespoons)
- Unbleached all-purpose flour (3 tablespoons)
- Olive oil cooking spray (2 to 4 spritzes, for tofu)
- Italian breadcrumbs (1/2 cup)
- Dried rosemary (1 tsp.)
- Dried thyme (1 tsp.)
- Black pepper (1/2 tsp.)
- Oregano (1/2 tsp.)

- Garlic powder (1/2 tsp.)
- Salt (1 tsp.)
- Onion powder (1 tsp.)

DAIRY:
- Shredded mozzarella cheese
- Grated parmesan cheese (1/2 cup)
- Butter (2 tbsp)

VEGETABLES, HERBS, AND SPICES:
- Yellow onion (1 small)
- Red bell pepper (1 small)
- Grilled corn kernels (2 cobs)
- Garlic (sliced thinly) (1 clove)
- Red onion (grated) (1 small)
- Spinach (1/3 cup packed)
- Zucchinis (2 thinly sliced)
- Cauliflower florets (3/4 cup)

PROTEIN:
- Extra-firm tofu (1 (16-ounce) package)
- Tempeh Bacon or store-bought vegan bacon (4 strips)
- Commercial vegan nuggets (4 pc)
- Lean ground turkey (1 lb)
- Beef (2 lb)

WEEK 1 MEAL PREPARATION

For making Bacon and Egg Sandwiches, take the tofu to drain and press it. First, cut the tofu into 3 equal pieces and then cut each tofu in half. There should be a total of 8 tofu slices. Now take a small bowl and whisk the milk, turmeric, nutritional yeast, black salt, and garlic powder and set aside. In a large bowl mix the flour and potato starch for dredging. Now dip each slice of tofu in the milk mixture and lightly coat each slice with flour mixture. Take an oil-sprayed air fryer basket and place the coated pieces of tofu in the basket. Spray the top of the tofus slightly and set the heat at 360 degrees Fahrenheit and cook each side for 6 minutes. Place two pieces of tofu eggs and one piece

of vegan bacon on each biscuit.

Prepare for Taco Wraps while bacon and egg sandwiches are cooking in the air fryer. First, preheat the air fryer to 400 degrees Fahrenheit. Now take a skillet and water saute the nuggets, onions, corn kernels, and bell peppers over medium heat. Fill up the tortillas with the veggies and nuggets. Place the tortillas inside the air fryer for 15 minutes or until crispy. Use mixed greens for garnish.

While the taco wraps are inside the air fryer for 15 minutes, prepare for Zucchini Parmesan Chips by cutting the zucchini. Take the zucchini and use a very sharp knife to cut as thinly as possible. Beat the eggs with a bit of water and a pinch of salt and pepper. Take a bowl and combine paprika, breadcrumbs, and cheese together. In the egg mixture dip slices of the zucchini and then into breadcrumbs until nicely coated. Mist-coat the zucchini slices using olive oil cooking spray and place them inside the air fryer in a single layer. Set the heat to 350 degrees Fahrenheit and cook for 8 minutes. Sprinkle the cooked slices with salt.

Prepare for Air-Fried Spinach Frittata by preheating the air fryer at 375 degrees Fahrenheit while Zucchini Parmesan Chips are cooking. Set a skillet over medium heat and add onion and oil. Cook until the onion is translucent and add spinach to saute until half cooked. In a bowl beat eggs and season using salt and pepper, add the spinach mixture in it. Cook the whole mixture in the air fryer for 8 minutes.

Prepare for Zucchini Turkey Burgers while the Air-Fried Spinach Frittata. In a bowl toss in the zucchini, ground turkey, salt, onion, garlic, pepper, and breadcrumbs and mix well. Make five patties using your hands and make sure the patties are not too thick. Preheat the air fryer to 375 degrees Fahrenheit and put the patties inside the air fryer in a single layer. Cook the patties for 7 minutes or until browned. Place the patties inside buns with ketchup and lettuce.

While the burger patties are inside the air fryer, prepare for Betty's Beef Roast. Preheat the air fryer to 330 degrees Fahrenheit. Now take a bowl and mix all the spices together. Use a brush to brush olive oil on the beef until well coated. Massage the spices over the beef for better flavor. Place the meat inside the air fryer and cook the first side for 30 minutes. After 30 minutes, turn over the meat and cook on the other side for 25 minutes.

Prepare Parmesan and garlic Cauliflower while the meat is inside the air fryer for an hour. First, preheat the air fryer to 250 degrees Fahrenheit. Now melt butter with the garlic on low heat for 5-10 minutes. Strain the garlic and add the cauliflower, salt, and parmesan. Bake it until golden brown, should take about 20 minutes.

Meal Plan Week 2

MONKEY BREAD

Prep time: 2 minutes | Cook time: 7 minutes | Serves 8

How to serve: Serve the monkey bread warm.
How to store: Store any leftover monkey bread in an airtight container at room temperature for up to 2 days. Reheat briefly in the air fryer for freshness.

CHEESE BURGER PATTIES

Prep time: 5 minutes | Cook time: 15 minutes | Serves 6

How to serve: Serve the cheeseburger patties hot.
How to store: Store any extra cheeseburger patties in the refrigerator in an airtight container for up to 2 days. Reheat in the air fryer or on a stovetop skillet.

AIR FRYER CINNAMON ROLLS

Prep time: 15 minutes | Cook time: 20 minutes | Serves 8

How to serve: Serve the cinnamon rolls drizzled in cream cheese glaze.
How to store: Store any leftover cinnamon rolls in the refrigerator for up to 2 days. Warm them in the air fryer or microwave before serving.

DIJON GARLIC PORK TENDERLOIN

Prep time: 20 minutes | Cook time: 15 minutes | Serves 6-8

How to serve: Serve the pork tenderloin hot.
How to store: Refrigerate any leftover pork tenderloin in an airtight container for up to 3 days. Reheat in the air fryer or oven for the best flavor.

CONFETTI SALMON BURGERS

Prep time: 5 minutes | Cook time: 27 minutes | Serves 4

How to serve: Serve the salmon burgers with lemon wedges.
How to store: Store any extra salmon burgers in the refrigerator in an airtight container for up to 2 days. Reheat in the air fryer or skillet.

BUFFALO CAULIFLOWER WINGS

Prep time: 5 minutes | Cook time: 15 minutes | Serves 6

How to serve: Serve the buffalo cauliflower wings warm.
How to store: Store any uneaten cauliflower wings in the refrigerator for up to 2 days.

Reheat in the air fryer for a crispy texture.

WEEK 2 SHOPPING LIST

PANTRY:
- non-fat Greek yogurt (1 cup)
- self-rising flour (1 cup)
- sugar (1 tsp)
- cinnamon (1/2 tsp)

GRAIN:
- cinnamon (1 1/2 tbsp)
- brown sugar (3/4 cup)
- melted coconut oil (1/4 cup)
- frozen bread dough, thawed (1 pound)
- breadcrumbs (1 cup)

FRUIT:
- lemons (2 small)

DAIRY:
- softened cream cheese (4 ounces)
- softened ghee (2 tbsp)

VEGETABLES, HERBS, AND SPICES:
- cayenne pepper (Pinch of)
- crushed garlic cloves (3)
- ground ginger (2 tbsp)
- Dijon mustard (2 tbsp)
- raw honey (2 tbsp)
- water (4 tbsp)
- salt (2 tsp)
- kosher salt (1/2 tsp)
- black pepper (1/2 tsp)
- minced scallion, white and light green parts only (1/4 cup)
- minced red bell pepper (1/4 cup)
- minced celery (1/4 cup)

NUTS AND SEEDS:
- almond flour (1 tablespoon)

PROTEIN:
- ground beef (1 lb)
- cooked fresh or canned salmon, flaked with a fork (14 ounces/400 g)
- pork tenderloin, sliced into 1-inch rounds (1 lb)

WEEK 2 MEAL PREPARATION

For making Monkey Bread take a medium bowl and combine the self-rising flour and yogurt together and form a dough. Transform the dough into a large ball and cut into fourths. Now shape the dough into flattened circular discs and cut into eight pieces, it should look like a pizza dough. Again remove the wedge from the discs and roll it to form into balls. Take a ziplock or plastic bag and combine sugar and cinnamon in it. Place the dough balls inside the bag and shake properly to coat the balls properly. Take a loaf pan and spray it with non-stick spray. Place the dough balls in the loaf pan and sprinkle lightly with the sugar and cinnamon mix. Set the air fryer at 375 degrees Fahrenheit and place the loaf pan inside the air fryer. Bake the bread for 7 minutes until well done.

While the bread is baking, prepare for Cheese Burger Patties by preheating your air fryer at 390 degrees Fahrenheit. Season the beef with salt and pepper and make six round-shaped patties. Place the patties inside the air fryer basket and fry for 10 minutes. After frying for 10 minutes, open the basket, place cheese slices on the patties, and let it cook for 1 minute.

Prepare for Air Fryer Cinnamon Rolls while the beef patties are cooking. Take the bread dough and shape it into a rectangle. Brush melted ghee over the dough and leave a 1-inch border near the edges. Mix together the cinnamon and sweetener and properly sprinkle over the dough. Make sure to roll the dough tightly and cut into 8 slices. Leave the slices to rise for 1-2 hours. To make the glaze, take the ingredients and mix them together until smooth. Once the rolls rise, place them inside the air fryer and cook for 5 minutes at 350 degrees Fahrenheit. Drizzle the rolls with cream cheese glaze.

While the dough is left to rise, prepare for Dijon Garlic Pork Tenderloin. Take the tenderloin and season all the sides with pepper and salt. In a small bowl combine the cayenne pepper, ginger, garlic, mustard, honey, and water until smooth. Now dip the pork rounds in the honey mixture and dip them into the breadcrumbs, making sure the pork rounds are well coated. Set the air fryer at 400 degrees Fahrenheit and place the coated pork rounds inside the air fryer. Cook for 10 minutes and then flip to cook for an extra 5 minutes until golden.

Prepare for Confetti Salmon Burgers while the pork is cooking. In a large bowl add vegetables, salmon, zest and juice of 1 lemon, eggs, crab boil seasoning, bread crumbs, salt, and pepper, and stir until well combined. Customize the mixture into 4 patties, each patty should weigh around 5 ounces. Leave it to chill for 15 minutes, until firm. Now spray the air fryer basket with oil and salmon patties on all sides. Set the heat to 400 degrees Fahrenheit and cook for 12 minutes. Make sure to flip them halfway though. Cook until the burgers are browned and well cooked.

While the burgers are left to chill, prepare for Buffalo Cauliflower Wings. Brush the air fryer basket using olive oil and set the fryer at 400 degrees Fahrenheit for 5 minutes. Cut the cauliflower into bite-size florets and set aside. In a large mixing bowl, add salt. Oil and hot sauce to whisk until well combined. Add the cauliflower pieces and toss until well combined. Now open the fryer and place the cauliflower florets in a single layer. Close the lid and cook until golden brown and crispy,

should take about 15 minutes. Make sure to shake halfway through to cook properly. Transfer the cauliflower florets to a serving plate and repeat the same process with the remaining cauliflower florets.

Meal Plan Week 3

COFFEE DONUTS

Prep time: 3 minutes | Cook Time: 17 minutes | Serves 6

How to serve: Serve the coffee donuts while warm.
How to store: Store any leftover donuts in an airtight container at room temperature for up to 2 days. Enjoy with a fresh cup of coffee.

EGG MUFFIN SANDWICH

Prep time: 3 minutes | Cook Time: 12 minutes | Serves 1

How to serve: Assemble the egg muffin sandwich with the cooked egg and bacon slices inside the muffin.
How to store: Store any extra sandwiches in the refrigerator for up to 2 days. Reheat gently in the air fryer or microwave.

COCONUT ORANGE CAKE

Prep time: 10 minutes | Cook time: 17 minutes | Serves 6

How to serve: Serve the coconut orange cake chilled.
How to store: Store any remaining cake in the refrigerator in an airtight container for up to 3 days. Serve cold for a refreshing dessert.

BUTTER WALNUT & RAISIN COOKIES

Prep time: 10 minutes | Cook time: 15 minutes | Serves 8

How to serve: Serve the cookies once they

have cooled.

How to store: Store any uneaten cookies in an airtight container at room temperature for up to 5 days. Enjoy with a glass of milk or your favorite beverage.

HONEY-DIJON TURKEY BREAST

Prep time: 5 minutes | Cook time: 30 minutes, plus 5 to 10 minutes to rest | Makes 8 slices

How to serve: Slice the turkey breast and serve with the honey-Dijon glaze.

How to store: Store any remaining turkey breast slices in the refrigerator in an airtight container for up to 3 days. Reheat gently in the air fryer or microwave for a warm, savory meal.

AIR FRYER MEATLOAF

Prep time: 10 minutes | Cook time: 45 minutes | Serves 8

How to serve: Slice the meatloaf and serve with the Dijon mustard and ketchup glaze.

How to store: Store any leftover meatloaf in the refrigerator in an airtight container for up to 3 days. Reheat in the air fryer or oven to maintain its delicious flavor and texture.

WEEK 3 SHOPPING LIST

PANTRY:

- flour (1 cup)
- sugar (1/4 cup)
- salt (1 tsp)
- baking powder (1 tsp)
- aquafaba (1 tbsp)
- sunflower oil (1 tbsp)
- coffee (1/4 cup)

GRAIN:

- shredded coconut (3/4 cup)
- almond flour (1 1/4 cups)
- nutmeg, grated (1/3 cup)
- baking powder (1/2 cup)

- breadcrumbs (1 cup)
- corn flour (1/2 cup)

DAIRY:

- butter (1 stick)

VEGETABLES, HERBS, AND SPICES:

- cayenne pepper (Pinch of)
- crushed garlic cloves (3)

NUTS AND SEEDS:

- walnuts, ground (1/3 cup)
- raisins (1/4 cup)

PROTEIN:

- boneless turkey breast (1 lb)
- ground lean beef (2 1/2 pounds)
- egg (1)
- eggs, beaten (2)

WEEK 3 MEAL PREPARATION

For making Coffee Donuts combine sugar, salt, baking powder, and flour in a large mixing bowl. Toss in the coffee, aquafaba, and sunflower oil and mix properly to form a dough. When the dough is formed, leave it in the refrigerator to rest. Set the air fryer's heat at 400 degrees Fahrenheit. Now remove the take out dough from the fridge and divide it. Knead each section into a doughnut. Place the donuts inside the air fryer and make sure to not overlap any donuts. Fry for 6 minutes and make sure to not shake the basket. Shaking the basket can destroy the well-shaped donuts.

While the donuts are baking, prepare for the Egg Muffin Sandwich. First, preheat the air fryer at 395 degrees Fahrenheit. Spray a ramekin using cooking spray and break an egg into the ramekin before transferring it to the basket. Make sure to keep each component separate. Cook for 6 minutes and after removing it from the fryer, let it cool down for 2 minutes. Make your sandwich by placing the egg and bacon slices on the base and topping with the other half muffin.

Prepare for Coconut Orange Cake while the muffins are baking in the air fryer. First, spritz the cake pan using cooking spray. Preheat the air fryer to 355 degrees Fahrenheit. Now combine butter with truvia and beat until fluffy. Add the eggs and keep mixing until smooth. Toss in nutmeg, flour, salt and slowly pour coconut milk. Lastly, add shredded coconut and orange jam to create a cake batter. Place the batter into the cake pan and bake the cake in the air fryer for 17 minutes. Once done, transfer the cake to a cooking rack.

While the cake is inside the air fryer, prepare Butter Walnut & Raisin Cookies by placing rum and raisin in a small bowl. Allow the ingredients to dry for 15 minutes. In another mixing dish, beat butter, Truvia, almond extract, and vanilla until fluffy. Now add both types of flour and ground almonds to the soaked raisin. Keep mixing until it forms a dough. Once the dough is formed, cover and store the dough inside the fridge for 20 minutes. At that time, preheat the air fryer to 330 degrees Fahrenheit and shape the dough into small cookies. Place the cookies inside the air fryer and gently press each cookie with a spoon, bake them for 15 minutes.

Prepare for Honey-Dijon Turkey Breast while the cookies are baking. Take a small bowl and add honey, dijon mustard, olive oil, garlic, butter, salt, and pepper, and which well. Brush the turkey breasts with honey mixture and place them inside the air fryer. Bake for 20 minutes and remove the turkey breasts. Brush using more honey mixture and bake for an extra 10 minutes until golden

brown. Before slicing, make sure to leave the turkey alone for 5-10 minutes.

While the turkey is cooking, prepare for Air Fryer Meatloaf by adding beef broth and breadcrumbs in a big bowl. Stir the mixture well and set it aside in a food processor. Add in onion, garlic, mushroom, and carrots and pulse on high mode until finely chopped. In a different bowl fold in soaked breadcrumbs, Worcestershire sauce, dijon mustard, lean ground beef, eggs, and salt. Use your hand to combine and make a loaf out of the ingredients. In the meantime, heat the air fryer at 390 degrees Fahrenheit, put the meatloaf in the air fryer, and cook for 45 minutes. In this 45 minutes, in a bowl add Dijon mustard, brown sugar, and ketchup and mix well. Use the mixture to glaze over the meatloaf.

Meal Plan Week 4

SOUTHWEST FRITTATA

Prep time: 10 minutes | Cook time: 18 to 20 minutes | Makes 6 slices

How to serve: Slice the frittata and serve warm.
How to store: Store any leftover frittata in the refrigerator in an airtight container for up to 2 days. Reheat gently in the air fryer or microwave before enjoying.

CRISPY BREAKFAST AVOCADO FRIES

Prep time: 10 minutes | Cook time: 6 minutes | Serves 2

How to serve: Serve the avocado fries with a sprinkle of lemon juice and Greek yogurt.
How to store: Store any remaining avocado fries in the refrigerator in an airtight container for up to 2 days. Reheat in the air fryer for a crispy texture.

APPLE PEACH CRANBERRY CRISP

Prep time: 10 minutes | Cook time: 12 minutes | Serves 8

How to serve: Serve the fruit crisp warm.
How to store: Store any uneaten crisp in the refrigerator in an airtight container for up to 3 days. Reheat in the air fryer or oven to enjoy the fruity goodness once more.

FRIED GARLIC CALAMARI

Prep time: 10 minutes | Cook time: 10 minutes | Serves 6

How to serve: Serve the fried calamari with garlic mayonnaise or lemon wedges.
How to store: Store any leftover calamari in the refrigerator in an airtight container for up to 2 days. Reheat in the air fryer or oven for a delightful, crispy snack.

PARMESAN BAKED SALMON

Prep time: 10 minutes | Cook time: 11 minutes | Serves 5

How to serve: Serve the Parmesan baked salmon immediately.
How to store: Store any remaining salmon in the refrigerator in an airtight container for up to 2 days. Reheat gently in the air fryer or oven to maintain its delicious flavor.

CHICKEN TENDERS WITH VEGGIES

Prep time: 10 minutes | Cook time: 18 to 20 minutes | Serves 4

How to serve: Serve the chicken tenders with the roasted carrots and red potatoes.
How to store: Store any leftover chicken tenders and veggies in the refrigerator in an airtight container for up to 2 days. Reheat in the air fryer or oven for a hearty meal.

PORK TRINOZA WRAPPED IN HAM

Prep time: 8 minutes | Cook time: 9 minutes | Serves 6

How to serve: Serve the pork Trinoza wrapped in ham after cooling.
How to store: Store any remaining pork Trinoza in the refrigerator in an airtight container for up to 2 days. Reheat in the air fryer or oven to enjoy this flavorful dish once more.

WEEK 4 SHOPPING LIST

PANTRY:
- Olive oil spray
- Honey (2 tablespoons)
- Brown sugar (⅓ cup)
- Flour (¼ cup)
- Oatmeal (½ cup)
- Softened butter (3 tablespoons)
- Coffee (¼ cup)

GRAIN:
- Whole-wheat flour (½ cup)
- Whole-wheat breadcrumbs (1 cup)

DAIRY:
- Cheddar-Monterey Jack cheese blend (1 cup)
- Butter (1 stick)
- Parmesan cheese, grated (½ cup)

VEGETABLES, HERBS, AND SPICES:
- Hot sauce (1 teaspoon)
- Salt (½ teaspoon)
- Ground black pepper (½ teaspoon)
- Ground cayenne pepper or chili powder (¼ teaspoon)
- Cayenne pepper (Pinch of)
- Crushed garlic cloves (3)
- Fresh parsley, chopped (¼ cup)
- Garlic cloves, minced (2)
- Olive oil (1 tablespoon)

NUTS AND SEEDS:

- Walnuts, ground (1/3 cup)

PROTEIN:

- Breakfast sausage, fully cooked and chopped (4 links)
- Eggs (5)
- Boneless turkey breast (1 lb)
- Ground lean beef (2 1/2 pounds)
- Calamari, cut into rings (1 lb)
- Fresh salmon filet (2 lbs)
- Chicken tenders (1 pound)
- Serrano ham, thinly sliced (6 pieces)
- Pork, halved (454 g)
- Mozzarella cheese, divided (4 slices)
- Fresh spinach leaves, divided (227 g)

WEEK 4 MEAL PREPARATION

For making Southwest Frittata, preheat the air fryer. Preheating the air fryer will help create a nice crust and decrease the cooking time as well. Take a nonstick 6 to 7-inch baking pan and spray it with olive oil. Add eggs, cheese, sausage, scallion, bell pepper, hot sauce, black pepper, cayenne pepper, and salt in a medium bowl and whisk to combine. Transfer the mixture to the nonstick pan and place the pan in the air fryer basket. Bake until the frittata is ready, should take about 18-20 minutes. Be careful to not overcook the frittata, it should stay dry and look golden outside.

Prepare for Crispy Breakfast Avocado Fries while the frittata is inside the air fryer by adding flour, cayenne pepper, salt, and pepper in a mixing bowl. Mix the ingredients well and add bread crumbs into another bowl. In a third bowl, beat the eggs. Now dredge the avocado slices in flour and dip them into the egg mixture, lastly dredge the breadcrumbs. Place the avocado fries in the air fryer and preheat the air fryer to 390

degrees Fahrenheit. Cook for 6 minutes and when done cooking, transfer the avocados into a serving platter. Sprinkle it with some lemon juice.

When the avocado is inside the air fryer, prepare for Apple Peach Cranberry Crisp. Take a 6 by 6 2-inch pan and combine the peaches, apple, cranberries, and honey and mix well. In a medium bowl, combine, flour, brown sugar, oatmeal, and butter and mix until the texture is crumbly. Take the mixture and sprinkle over the fruit in the pan. Bake it until the fruit is bubbly and the topping is golden brown, should take about 10-12 minutes.

Prepare for Fried Garlic Calamari while the cranberry crisps are baking. Take the calamari rings and coat them with flour. Dip the calamari in the egg and mashed garlic mixture. Dip them in the pork rinds and leave the calamari rings inside the fridge for 2 hours. Next, place them into the air fryer and apply the oil carefully. Make sure to set the temperature to 380 degrees Fahrenheit and cook for 10 minutes.

While the calamari is cooking, prepare for Parmesan Baked Salmon by preheating your air fryer to 300 degrees Fahrenheit. On a foil, place the salmon with skin side down and cover with more foil. Place it in the air fryer and cook for 10 minutes. After cooking, open the foil and sprinkle the salmon with cheese, garlic, pepper, salt, and parsley. Cook for an additional 1 minute.

Take a medium bowl for preparing Chicken Tenders with Veggies while the salmon is cooking. In that medium bowl, toss the chicken tenders with salt, honey, and pepper. Take a shallow bowl and combine the bread crumbs, olive oil, thyme and mix properly.

Coat the tenders with bread crumbs and press firmly on the meat. In the air fryer basket, place the carrots and potatoes and top with the chicken tenders. Set the temperature to 165 degrees Fahrenheit and roast for 18 to 20 minutes till the vegetables are tender. Make sure to shake the basket halfway during the cooking time.

While the chicken tender is cooking inside the air fryer, prepare for Pork Trinoza Wrapped In Ham. On baking paper, place 3 pieces of ham and they should slightly overlap each other. Place 1 half of the pork in hand and repeat with the other half. Use salt and pepper to season the inside of the pork rolls. Place cheese, sun-dried tomatoes, and half of the spinach on top of the pork loin. Make sure to leave a 13 mm border on all sides. Now carefully roll the filets around the filling and tie using a kitchen cord. Repeat the same process for other pork steaks and store them in the fridge. Brush the olive oil on each steak and place them in the preheated air fryer. Select the steak mode and set the timer for 9 minutes. After cooking, leave the steak to cool down before cutting.

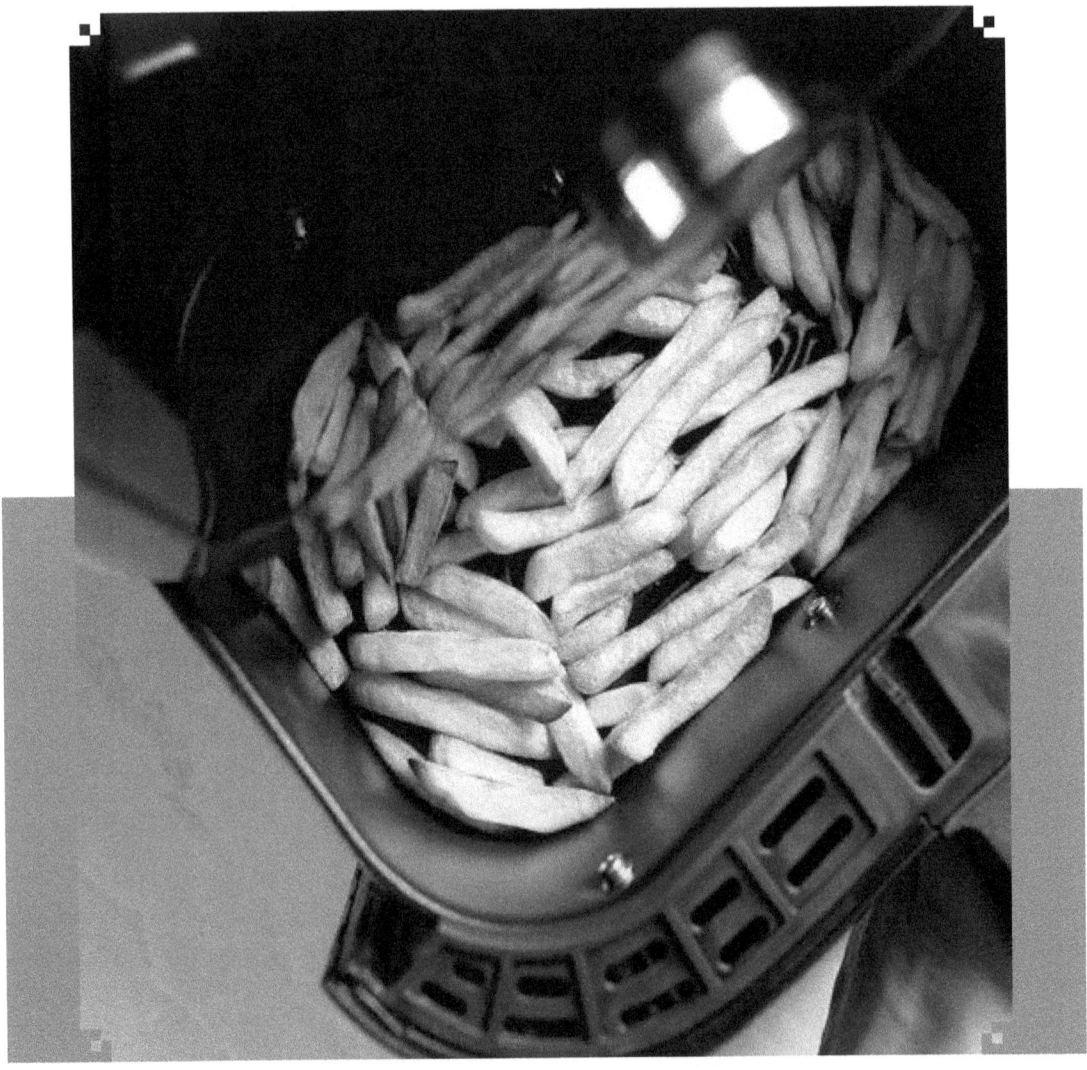

Chapter 2

Breakfasts

Bacon and Egg Sandwiches

Prep time: 10 minutes | Cook time:12 minutes |Serves 4

- 1 (16-ounce) package extra-firm tofu
- 1/2 cup soymilk
- 1/4 cup plus 2 tablespoons nutritional yeast
- 1 teaspoon garlic powder
- 1/2 teaspoon black salt
- 1 tablespoon potato starch
- 2 to 4 spritzes canola oil spray
- 4 strips Tempeh Bacon or store-bought vegan bacon
- 4 Fried Biscuits or store-bought vegan biscuits

1. Drain and press the tofu (see the sidebar here for instructions). Cut the tofu into 4 equal pieces. Then cut each piece in half, for a total of 8 slices.
2. In a small bowl, whisk together the milk, nutritional yeast, turmeric, garlic powder, and black salt until combined. Set aside.
3. Mix the flour and potato starch together on a large plate for dredging. Dip each piece of tofu in the milk mixture. Then lightly coat each piece with the flour mixture.
4. Spray the air fryer basket with the canola oil. Place the coated pieces of tofu in the basket and lightly spray the top of the tofu. Cook at 360°F for 6 minutes. Flip the tofu slices and cook for 6 minutes longer. Place two tofu eggs and one piece of vegan bacon on each biscuit.

Monkey Bread

Prep time: 2 minutes | Cook time: 7 minutes | Serves 8

- 1 cup non-fat Greek yogurt
- 1 cup self-rising flour
- 1 tsp. sugar
- ½ tsp. cinnamon

1. Combine in a medium bowl the self-rising flour and yogurt; mix well to form into dough.
2. Custom the dough into a large ball and cut into fourths.
3. Remove each dough wedge to shape into a flattened circular disc, and then cut into eight pieces, similar to a pizza. Remove each wedge from the disc and roll it to form into balls.
4. Combine cinnamon and sugar in a Ziploc or resealable plastic bag. Add the dough balls and seal the bag; shake to coat the balls well. Prepare a mini loaf pan by lightly misting it with non-stick spray.
5. Arrange the dough balls in the pan and sprinkle lightly with the sugar-cinnamon mix.
6. Put the loaf pan inside the air fryer. Bake the bread for 7 minutes, at 375°F. Let cool.

Grilled Cheese Sandwiches

Prep time: 2 minutes | Cook time: 7 minutes | Serves 2

- 4 slices American cheese
- 4 slices sandwich bread
- Pat Butter

1. Warm your air fryer to 360°F. Fill the center of 2 bread slices with two slices of American cheese.
2. Binge an even layer of butter on each side of the sandwich and position it in the hamper of your air fryer in a single layer. Insert toothpicks on the corners of each sandwich to seal.
3. Air-fries the sandwiches for 4 minutes, flipping once, and cook for another 3 minutes until toasted.

Chocolate & Zucchini Muffins

Prep time: 5 minutes | Cook time:36 minutes |Serves 1

- 1 tbsp ground flaxseed
- 3 tbsp water
- ½ cup all-purpose flour
- ¼ cup whole wheat pastry flour
- ¼ cup unsweetened cocoa powder
- ¼ tsp baking soda
- ¼ tsp kosher salt
- ¼ tsp ground cinnamon
- ½ cup granulated sugar
- ¼ cup canola oil
- ½ tsp pure vanilla extract
- ½ tsp freshly squeezed lemon juice
- ¾ cup grated zucchini
- ½ cup vegan chocolate chips

1. Set the air fryer temp to 270°F. Spray 12 silicone muffin cups with nonstick cooking spray. Set aside.
2. In a small bowl, combine the flaxseed and water.
3. In a large bowl, whisk together the all-purpose flour, whole wheat pastry flour, cocoa powder, baking soda, salt, and cinnamon. Add the sugar, canola oil, vanilla extract, lemon juice, and flaxseed mixture. Mix well. Fold in the zucchini and chocolate chips. Place the batter into the muffin cups.
4. Working in batches, place 6 muffin cups in the fryer basket and bake until a toothpick comes out clean from the center of a muffin, about 15 to 18 minutes.
5. Remove the cups from the fryer basket and allow the muffins to cool for 10 minutes before serving.

Taco Wraps

Prep time: 5 minutes | Cook Time: 25 minutes | Serves 4

- 1 tbsp. water
- 4 pc commercial vegan nuggets, chopped
- 1 small yellow onion, diced
- 1 small red bell pepper, chopped
- 2 cobs grilled corn kernels
- 4 large corn tortillas
- Mixed greens for garnish

1. Pre-heat your Air Fryer at 400°F.
2. Over a medium heat, water-sauté the nuggets with the onions, corn kernels and bell peppers in a skillet, then remove from the heat.
3. Fill the tortillas with the nuggets and vegetables and fold them up. Transfer to the inside of the fryer and cook for 15 minutes. Once crispy, serve immediately, garnished with the mixed greens.

Southwest Frittata

Prep time: 10 minutes | Cook time: 18 to 20 minutes|Makes 6 slices

- Olive oil spray
- 4 eggs
- 1 scallion, finely chopped
- 1 teaspoon hot sauce
- ½ teaspoon salt
- ½ teaspoon ground black pepper
- ¼ teaspoon ground cayenne pepper or chili powder

1. Preheat the air fryer. (This will help create a nice crust and decrease the cooking time a bit to keep the frittata from getting too brown on top.)
2. Spray a nonstick 6- or 7-inch baking pan with olive oil.
3. In a medium bowl, add the eggs, sausage, cheese, bell pepper, scallion, hot sauce, salt, black pepper, and cayenne pepper, and whisk to combine.
4. Slice, and serve warm.

Indian Masala Omelet

Prep time: 10 minutes | Cook time:12 minutes |Serves 2

- 4 large eggs
- ½ cup diced onion
- ½ cup diced tomato
- ¼ cup chopped fresh cilantro
- 1 jalapeño, seeded and finely chopped
- ½ teaspoon ground turmeric
- ½ teaspoon kosher salt
- ½ teaspoon cayenne pepper
- Olive oil for greasing the pan

1. In a large bowl, beat the eggs. Stir in the onion, tomato, cilantro, jalapeño, turmeric, salt, and cayenne.
2. Generously grease a 3-cup Bundt pan. (Be sure to grease the pan well—the proteins in eggs stick something fierce. and do not use a round baking pan. The hole in the center of a Bundt pan allows hot air to circulate through the middle of the omelet so that it will cook at the same rate as the outside.)
3. Pour the egg mixture into the prepared pan. Place the pan in the air fryer basket. Set the air fryer to 250°F for 12 minutes, or until the eggs are cooked through. Carefully unmold and cut the omelet into four pieces (2 pieces per serving).

Crispy Breakfast Avocado Fries

Prep time: 10 minutes | Cook time: 6 minutes | Serves 2

- 2 eggs, beaten
- 2 large avocados, peeled, pitted, cut into 8 slices each
- ¼ tsp. pepper
- ½ tsp. cayenne pepper
- Salt, to taste
- ½ a lemon, Juice
- ½ cup whole-wheat flour
- 1 cup whole-wheat breadcrumbs
- Greek yogurt to serve

1. Add flour, salt, pepper, and cayenne pepper to bowl and mix. Add bread crumbs into another bowl. Beat eggs in a third bowl.
2. First, dredge the avocado slices in the flour mixture. Next, dip them into the egg mixture, and finally dredge them in the breadcrumbs. Place avocado fries into the air fryer basket. Preheat the air fryer to 390°F.
3. Place the air fryer basket into the air fryer and cook for 6 minutes.
4. When Cooking Time is completed, transfer the avocado fries onto a serving platter.
5. Sprinkle with lemon juice and serve with Greek yogurt.

Granola-Stuffed Baked Apples

Prep time: 5 minutes | Cook time:20 minutes |Serves 2

- 4 Granny Smith or other firm apples
- 1 cup (100 g) granola
- 2 tablespoons (19 g) light brown sugar
- 3/4 teaspoon cinnamon
- 2 tablespoons (28 g) unsalted butter, melted
- 1 cup (240 ml) water or apple juice

1. Working one apple at a time, cut a circle around the apple stem and scoop out the core, taking care not to cut all the way through to the bottom. (This should leave an empty cavity in the middle of the apple for the granola.) Repeat with the remaining apples.
2. In a small bowl, combine the granola, brown sugar, and cinnamon. Pour the melted butter over the ingredients and stir with a fork. Divide the granola mixture among the apples, packing it tightly into the empty cavity.
3. Place the apples in the cake pan insert for the air fryer. Pour the water or juice around the apples. Bake at 350°F (180°C) for 20 minutes until the apples are soft all the way through. (If the granola begins to scorch before the apples are fully cooked, cover the top of the apples with a small piece of aluminum foil.)
4. Serve warm with a dollop of crème fraîche or yogurt, if desired.

Egg Muffin Sandwich

Prep time: 3 minutes | Cook Time: 12 minutes | Serves 1

- 1 egg
- 2 slices bacon
- 1 English muffin

1. Pre-heat your Air Fryer at 395°F.
2. Take a ramekin and spritz it with cooking spray. Break an egg into the ramekin before transferring it to the basket of your fryer, along with the English muffin and bacon slices, keeping each component separate.
3. Allow to cook for 6 minutes. After removing from the fryer, allow to cool for around two minutes. Halve the muffin.
4. Create your sandwich by arranging the egg and bacon slices on the base and topping with the other half of the muffin.

Mexican Breakfast Pepper Rings

Prep time: 5 minutes | Cook time:10 minutes |Serves 4

- Olive oil
- 1 large red, yellow, or orange bell pepper, cut into four ¾-inch rings
- 4 eggs
- Salt
- Freshly ground black pepper
- 2 teaspoons salsa

1. Lightly spray a small round air fryer–friendly pan with olive oil.
2. Place 2 bell pepper rings on the pan. Crack one egg into each bell pepper ring. Season with salt and black pepper.
3. Spoon ½ teaspoon of salsa on top of each egg.
4. Place the pan in the fryer basket. Air fry until the yolk is slightly runny, 5 to 6 minutes or until the yolk is fully cooked, 8 to 10 minutes.
5. Repeat with the remaining 2 pepper rings. Serve hot.

Coffee Donuts

Prep time: 3 minutes | Cook Time: 17 minutes | Serves 6

- 1 cup flour
- ¼ cup sugar
- ½ tsp. salt
- 1 tsp. baking powder
- 1 tbsp. aquafaba
- 1 tbsp. sunflower oil
- ¼ cup coffee

1. In a large bowl, combine the sugar, salt, flour, and baking powder.
2. Add in the coffee, aquafaba, and sunflower oil and mix until a dough is formed. Leave the dough to rest in and the refrigerator.
3. Set your Air Fryer at 400°F to heat up.
4. Remove the dough from the fridge and divide up, kneading each section into a doughnut.
5. Put the doughnuts inside the Air Fryer, ensuring not to overlap any. Fry for 6 minutes. Do not shake the basket, to make sure the doughnuts hold their shape.

Harissa Shakshuka

Prep time: 15 minutes | Cook time:15 minutes |Serves 4

For the Harissa
- ½ cup olive oil
- 6 cloves garlic, minced
- 2 tablespoons smoked paprika
- 1 tablespoon ground coriander
- 1 tablespoon ground cumin
- 1 teaspoon ground caraway
- 1 teaspoon kosher salt
- ½ to 1 teaspoon cayenne pepper

For the Shakshuka
- 1 cup canned diced tomatoes with their liquid
- 4 large eggs
- Chopped fresh parsley (optional)
- Black pepper (optional)

For the harissa:
1. In a medium microwave-safe bowl, combine all the ingredients. Microwave on high for 1 minute, stirring halfway through the cooking time. (You can also heat this on the stovetop until the oil is hot and bubbling. Or, if you must use your air fryer for everything, cook in the air fryer at 350°F for 5 to 6 minutes, or until the paste is heated through.)

For the shakshuka:
2. In a 6 × 3-inch round heatproof pan, combine the tomatoes with 1 teaspoon of the harissa and stir until well combined. Taste and add more harissa if you want the sauce to be spicier.
3. Carefully crack the eggs into the tomato mixture, taking care to not break the yolks. Cover the pan with foil and place in the air fryer basket. Set the air fryer to 350°F for 15 minutes. Remove the foil. For a runny yolk, cook for an additional 3 minutes; for a more set yolk, cook an additional 5 minutes.
4. Garnish with fresh parsley and black pepper, if desired.

Air Fryer Bacon

Prep time: 2 minutes | Cook time: 10 minutes | Serves 5

- 5 slices (thick-cut) bacon

1. Lay the bacon slices into your air fryer basket, at least 1 inch apart, to cook. Heat the air fryer at 390°F. Cook bacon for 10 minutes until crispy.
2. Drain on a kitchen napkin before serving.

Black Bean Burger Burritos

Prep time: 20 minutes | Cook time:10 minutes |Serves 1

- 4 black bean burgers
- sriracha chili sauce
- 4 large flour tortillas
- baby spinach
- 1 avocado, diced

1. Set the air fryer temp to 380°F.
2. Place the black bean burgers in the fryer basket and cook for 4 minutes per side.
3. Remove the burgers from the fryer basket and roughly chop. Spread the chili sauce on the tortillas and top with equal amounts of spinach, avocado, and burger. Wrap the tortillas around the filling.
4. Place the burritos in the fryer basket and cook until the tortillas are toasted, about 2 minutes.
5. Remove the burritos from the fryer basket and cut in half. Serve immediately or wrap them in aluminum foil for an on-the-go meal.

Eggs in a Basket

Prep time: 5 minutes | Cook time:8 minutes |Serves 1

- 1 thick slice country, sourdough, or Italian bread
- 2 tablespoons (28 g) unsalted butter, melted
- 1 egg
- Kosher salt and pepper to taste

1. Brush the bottom of the air fryer cake pan insert and both sides of the bread with melted butter. Using a small round cookie or biscuit cutter, cut a hole out of the middle of the bread and set it aside.
2. Place the slice of bread in the air fryer cake pan insert. Crack the egg into the hole in the bread, taking care not to break the yolk. Season with salt and pepper. Place the cut-out bread hole next to the slice of bread. Place the cake pan insert into the air fryer.
3. Bake at 300°F (150°C) for 6 to 8 minutes until the egg white is set but the yolk is still runny. Using a silicone spatula, remove the bread slice to a plate. Serve with the cut-out bread circle on the side or place it on top of the egg.

Two-Ingredient Cream Biscuits

Prep time: 10 minutes | Cook time:21 minutes |Serves 2

- 1 cup (125 g) self-rising flour
- 1/2 cup (120 ml) plus 1 tablespoon (15 ml) heavy cream
- Vegetable oil for spraying
- 2 tablespoons (28 g) unsalted butter, melted (optional)

1. Place the flour in a medium bowl and whisk to remove any lumps. Make a well in the center of the flour. While stirring with a fork, slowly pour in the cream in a steady stream. Continue to stir until the dough has mostly come together. with your hands, gather the dough, incorporating any dry flour, and form it into a ball.
2. Preheat the air fryer to 325°F (170°C) for 3 minutes. Spray the air fryer basket with oil to prevent sticking. Place the biscuits in the air fryer basket so that they are barely touching. Cook for 15 to 18 minutes until the tops are browned and the insides fully cooked. Remove the biscuits to a plate, brush the tops with melted butter, if using, and serve.

Bistro Wedges

Prep time: 5 minutes | Cook Time: 15 minutes | Serves 4

- 1 lb. fingerling potatoes, cut into wedges
- 1 tsp. extra virgin olive oil
- ½ tsp. garlic powder
- Salt and pepper to taste
- ½ cup raw cashews, soaked in water overnight
- ½ tsp. ground turmeric
- ½ tsp. paprika
- 1 tbsp. nutritional yeast
- 1 tsp. fresh lemon juice
- 2 tbsp. to ¼ cup water

1. Pre-heat your Air Fryer at 400°F.
2. In a bowl, toss together the potato wedges, olive oil, garlic powder, and salt and pepper, making sure to coat the potatoes well.
3. Transfer the potatoes to the basket of your fryer and fry for 10 minutes.
4. In the meantime, prepare the cheese sauce. Pulse the cashews, turmeric, paprika, nutritional yeast, lemon juice, and water together in a food processor. Add more water to achieve your desired consistency.
5. When the potatoes are finished cooking, move them to a bowl that is small enough to fit inside the fryer and add the cheese sauce on top. Cook for an additional 3 minutes.

Breakfast Cod Nuggets

Prep time: 10 minutes | Cook time: 10 minutes | Serves 4

- 1 lb. cod

For Breading:
- 2 eggs, beaten
- 2 tbsp. olive oil
- 1 cup almond flour
- ¾ cup breadcrumbs

- 1 tsp. dried parsley
- Pinch sea salt
- ½ tsp. black pepper

1. Preheat the air fryer to 390°F.
2. Cut the cod into strips about 1-inch by 2-inches. Blend breadcrumbs, olive oil, salt, parsley, and pepper in a food processor.
3. In 3 separate bowls, add breadcrumbs, eggs, and flour. Place each piece of fish into flour, then the eggs, and the breadcrumbs. Add pieces of cod to the air fryer basket and cook for 10 minutes. Serve warm.

Puffed Egg Tarts

Prep time: 10 minutes | Cook time: 17 to 20 minutes| Makes 2 tarts

- ⅓ sheet frozen puff pastry, thawed
- ½ cup shredded Cheddar cheese
- 2 eggs
- ¼ teaspoon salt
- 1 teaspoon minced fresh parsley, for garnish (optional)

1. Lay the sheet of puff pastry on a piece of parchment paper and cut in half.
2. Transfer the 2 squares of puff pastry to the air fryer basket, keeping them on the parchment paper, and bake for 10 minutes, or until the pastry is golden brown.
3. Open the basket and use a metal spoon to press down the center of each pastry square to make a well.
4. Divide the cheese equally between the cooked pastries.
5. Carefully crack an egg on top of the cheese on each pastry, and sprinkle ⅛ teaspoon of salt over each.
6. Bake for an additional 7 to 10 minutes, or until the eggs are cooked through.
7. Sprinkle with parsley (if using), and serve.

Easy Cheesy Egg Cups

Prep time: 7 minutes | Cook time: 4 minutes | Makes 6 egg cups

- 4 eggs
- 2 cups Cheddar cheese
- ½ cup 2% cottage cheese
- ¼ cup heavy (whipping) cream
- 1 tablespoon bacon bits
- ½ teaspoon salt
- ½ teaspoon ground black pepper

1. In a blender, combine the eggs, Cheddar cheese, cottage cheese, cream, bacon bits, salt, and pepper, and blend on high for 20 seconds.
2. Pour the egg batter into a silicone muffin mold. Place inside the air fryer basket, bake for 4 minutes, until the muffins are no longer moist on top, and serve.

Tofu Rancheros

Prep time: 10 minutes | Cook time:5 minutes |Serves 1

- 2 cups crumbled firm tofu
- 2 tsp Dijon mustard
- 1 tsp nutritional yeast
- ½ tsp ground turmeric
- ½ tsp kosher salt

For Serving
- 1 cup black beans
- ½ cup thinly sliced radishes
- 1 avocado, sliced
- chopped fresh cilantro
- 4 medium corn tortillas, warmed
- hot sauce (Frank's RedHot recommended) (optional)

1. Set the air fryer temp to 400°F.
2. In a baking dish, combine the tofu, mustard, nutritional yeast, turmeric, and salt. Mix well.

3. Place the dish in the fryer basket and cook until warmed, about 5 minutes.
4. Remove the dish from the fryer basket and stir the ingredients. Place the tofu mixture, black beans, radishes, avocado, cilantro, and hot sauce (if using) on the tortillas. Serve immediately.

English Builder's Breakfast

Prep time: 5 minutes | Cook Time: 30 minutes | Serves 2

- 1 cup potatoes, sliced and diced
- 2 cups beans in tomato sauce
- 2 eggs
- 1 tbsp. olive oil
- 1 sausage
- Salt to taste

1. Set your Air Fryer at 390°F and allow to warm.
2. Break the eggs onto an fryer-safe dish and sprinkle on some salt.
3. Lay the beans on the dish, next to the eggs.
4. In a bowl small enough to fit inside your fryer, coat the potatoes with the olive oil. Sprinkle on the salt, as desired.
5. Slice up the sausage and throw the slices in on top of the beans and eggs. Resume cooking for another 5 minutes. Serve with the potatoes, as well as toast and coffee if desired.

Chapter 3

Poultry

Italian Chicken and Veggies

Prep time: 10 minutes | Cook time:30 minutes |Serves 4

- ¾ cup balsamic vinaigrette dressing, divided
- 1 pound boneless, skinless chicken tenderloins
- Olive oil
- 1 pound fresh green beans, trimmed
- 1 pint grape tomatoes

1. Place ½ cup of the balsamic vinaigrette dressing and the chicken in a large zip-top plastic bag, seal, and refrigerate for at least 1 hour or up to overnight.
2. In a large bowl, mix together the green beans, tomatoes, and the remaining ¼ cup of balsamic vinaigrette dressing until well coated.
3. Spray the fryer basket lightly with oil. Place the vegetables in the fryer basket. Reserve any remaining vinaigrette.
4. Air fry for 8 minutes. Shake the basket and continue to cook until the beans are crisp but tender, and the tomatoes are soft and slightly charred, an additional 5 to 7 minutes.
5. Wipe the fryer basket with a paper towel and spray lightly with olive oil.
6. Air fry for 7 minutes. Flip the chicken over, baste with some of the remaining vinaigrette, and cook until the chicken reaches an internal temperature of 165°F, an additional 5 to 8 minutes.
7. Serve the chicken and veggies together.

Italian Chicken Thighs

Prep time: 5 minutes | Cook Time: 25 minutes | Serves 4

- 4 skin-on bone-in chicken thighs
- 2 tbsp. unsalted butter, melted
- 3 tsp. Italian herbs
- ½ tsp. garlic powder
- ¼ tsp. onion powder

1. Using a brush, coat the chicken thighs with the melted butter. Combine the herbs with the garlic powder and onion powder, then massage into the chicken thighs. Place the thighs in the fryer.
2. Cook at 380°F for 20 minutes, turning the chicken halfway through to cook on the other side.
3. When the thighs have achieved a golden color, test the temperature with a meat thermometer. Once they have reached 165°F, remove from the fryer and serve.

No-Breaded Turkey Breast

Prep time: 5 minutes | Cook time: 40-60 minutes | Serves 10

- Turkey breast: 4 pounds, ribs removed, bone with skin
- Olive oil: 1 tablespoon
- Salt: 2 teaspoons
- Dry turkey seasoning (without salt): half tsp.

1. Rub half tbsp of olive oil over turkey breast. Sprinkle salt, turkey seasoning on both sides of turkey breast with half tbsp of olive oil.
2. Let the air fryer preheat at 350 F. put turkey skin side down in air fryer and cook for 20 minutes until the turkey's temperature reaches 160 F for half an hour to 40 minutes.
3. Let it sit for ten minutes before slicing.

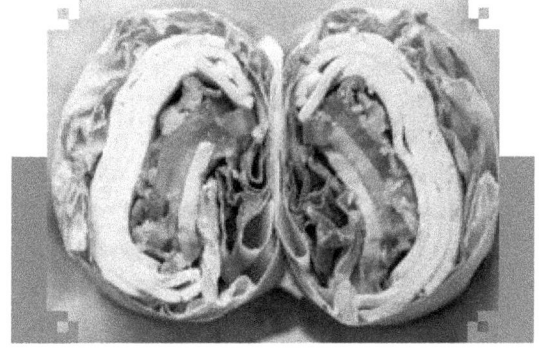

Cilantro Chicken Kebabs

Prep time: 20 minutes | Cook time:10 minutes |Serves 4

For the Chutney
- ½ cup unsweetened shredded coconut
- ½ cup hot water
- 2 cups fresh cilantro leaves, roughly chopped
- ¼ cup fresh mint leaves, roughly chopped
- 6 cloves garlic, roughly chopped
- 1 jalapeño, seeded and roughly chopped
- ¼ to ¾ cup water, as needed
- Juice of 1 lemon

For the Chicken
- 1 pound boneless, skinless chicken thighs, cut crosswise into thirds
- Olive oil spray

1. For the chutney: In a blender or food processor, combine the coconut and hot water; set aside to soak for 5 minutes.
2. To the processor, add the cilantro, mint, garlic, and jalapeño, along with ¼ cup water. Blend at low speed, stopping occasionally to scrape down the sides. Add the lemon juice. with the blender or processor running, add only enough additional water to keep the contents moving. Turn the blender to high once the contents are moving freely and blend until the mixture is puréed.
3. For the chicken: Place the chicken pieces in a large bowl. Add ¼ cup of the chutney and mix well to coat. Set aside the remaining chutney to use as a dip. Marinate the chicken for 15 minutes at room temperature.
4. Spray the air fryer basket with olive oil spray. Arrange the chicken in the air fryer basket. Set the air fryer to 350°F for 10 minutes. Use a meat thermometer to ensure that the chicken has reached an internal temperature of 165°F.
5. Serve the chicken with the remaining chutney.

Teriyaki Chicken Wings

Prep time: 5 minutes | Cook Time: 40 minutes | Serves 4

- ¼ tsp. ground ginger
- 2 tsp. minced garlic
- ½ cup sugar-free teriyaki sauce
- 2 lb. chicken wings
- 2 tsp. baking powder

1. In a small bowl, combine together the ginger, garlic, and teriyaki sauce. Place the chicken wings in a separate, larger bowl and pour the mixture over them. Toss to coat until the chicken is well covered.
2. Refrigerate for at least an hour.
3. Remove the marinated wings from the fridge and add the baking powder, tossing again to coat. Then place the chicken in the basket of your air fryer.
4. Cook for 25 minutes at 400°F, giving the basket a shake intermittently throughout the cooking time.
5. When the wings are 165°F and golden in color, remove from the fryer and serve immediately.

Buttermilk Fried Chicken and Waffles

Prep time: 10 minutes | Cook time: 25 minutes |Serves 4

- 4 small boneless, skinless chicken breasts totaling approximately 2 pounds (910 g)
- 1/2 cup (63 g) all-purpose flour
- 1 teaspoon kosher salt
- 1/2 teaspoon cayenne pepper
- 1 egg
- 2 tablespoons (30 ml) buttermilk
- Dash hot sauce
- 11/2 cups (75 g) panko bread crumbs
- Vegetable oil for spraying
- 13/4 cups (219 g) all-purpose flour
- 2 teaspoons baking powder
- 1 teaspoon granulated sugar
- 1 teaspoon baking soda
- 1 teaspoon kosher salt
- 13/4 cups (420 ml) buttermilk
- 2 eggs
- 1/2 cup (112 g, or 1 stick) unsalted butter, melted and cooled
- Maple syrup or honey to serve

1. To make the chicken, cut each chicken breast in half lengthwise to make 2 long chicken tenders. Whisk together the flour, salt, and cayenne pepper on a large plate. Beat the egg with the buttermilk and hot sauce in a large, shallow bowl. Place the panko in a separate shallow bowl or pie plate.
2. Dredge the chicken tenders in the flour, shaking off any excess, then dip them in the egg mixture. Dredge the chicken tenders in the panko, making sure to coat them completely. Shake off any excess panko. Place the battered chicken tenders on a plate.
3. Preheat the air fryer to 375°F (190°C). Spray the basket lightly with oil. Arrange half the chicken tenders in the basket of the air fryer and spray the tops with oil. Cook at 375°F (190°C) until the top side of the tenders is browned and crispy, 8 to 10 minutes. Flip the tenders and spray the second side with oil. Cook until the second side is browned and crispy and the internal temperature reaches 165°F (71°C), another 8 to 10 minutes. Remove the first batch of tenders and keep it warm. Cook the second batch in the same manner.
4. While the tenders are cooking, make the waffles. In a large bowl, whisk together the flour, baking powder, sugar, baking soda, and salt. In a separate bowl, whisk together the buttermilk, eggs, and melted butter, reserving a small amount of butter to brush on the waffle iron. Add the wet ingredients to the dry ingredients and stir with a fork until just combined. Allow the batter to rest for at least 5 minutes. Brush the waffle iron with reserved melted butter and preheat according to the manufacturer's instructions. Scoop 1/3 to 1/2 cup (85 to 125 g) of batter into each grid of the waffle iron and cook according to your waffle iron's instructions. (You should be able to make 8 waffles.)
5. To serve, place 2 chicken tenders on top of 1 or 2 waffles, depending on the person's appetite. Serve with maple syrup or honey and additional hot sauce.

Chicken Parmesan

Prep time: 5 minutes | Cook time: 14 minutes |Serves 4

- 1 egg
- 1 tablespoon (14 g) mayonnaise
- 1 cup (50 g) panko bread crumbs
- 1/2 cup (75 g) freshly grated Parmesan cheese
- 1 teaspoon Italian seasoning
- 1 pound (455 g) boneless, skinless hand-filleted chicken breasts or regular breasts sliced in half crosswise to create 4 thin breasts
- Vegetable oil for spraying
- 1/4 cup (61 g) Marinara Sauce
- 6 tablespoons (45 g) grated mozzarella cheese

1. Mix the egg and mayonnaise in a shallow bowl until smooth. In another bowl, combine the panko, Parmesan cheese, and Italian seasoning. Dip each piece of chicken in the mayonnaise mixture, shaking off any excess, then dredge in the panko mixture until both sides are coated. Place the breaded chicken on a plate or rack.
2. Preheat the air fryer to 350°F (180°C) for 3 minutes. Spray the basket of the air fryer with oil and place 2 pieces of chicken in the basket. Spray the chicken cutlets with oil. Cook the cutlets for 6 minutes, then turn them over. Top each piece of chicken with 1 tablespoon (15 g) of marinara sauce and 1^1/2 tablespoons (11 g) of grated mozzarella cheese. Cook the chicken until the cheese is melted, about 3 additional minutes.
3. Remove the cooked chicken to a serving dish and keep warm. Cook the remaining pieces of chicken in the same manner. Serve warm with pasta on the side.

Chicken Taco Crunch Surprise Wraps

Prep time: 10 minutes | Cook time: 8 minutes |Makes 2 wraps

- 2 (12-inch) flour tortillas at room temperature
- ½ cup refried beans
- 2 cups seasoned and cooked rotisserie chicken
- 1 tomato, diced
- 4 ounces nacho cheese
- ½ cup shredded lettuce
- 1 cup Mexican-blend cheese
- ½ cup sour cream, plus more for serving
- 2 tostada shells
- Olive oil spray
- Hot sauce, for serving (optional)

1. Preheat the air fryer to .
2. In the center of each flour tortilla, spread about half of the refried beans, chicken, tomato, nacho cheese, lettuce, Mexican-blend cheese, and sour cream.
3. Top each with a tostada shell, then wrap the edges of the flour tortilla up and over the center, sort of like wrapping a round gift with wrapping paper.
4. Spray both sides of one wrap with olive oil, and place it folded-side down in the air fryer. Spray with more olive oil, and bake for 2 minutes.
5. Remove the fryer basket, and flip the wrap over. Return to the fryer and bake for an additional 2 minutes, until golden.
6. Repeat with the second wrap.
7. Serve with additional sour cream and hot sauce (if using).

Zucchini Turkey Burgers

Prep time: 10 minutes | Cook time: 10 minutes | Serves 5

- 1/4 cup (seasoned) gluten-free breadcrumbs
- 1 cup grated zucchini
- 1 tbsp. (grated) red onion
- 4 cups lean ground turkey
- 1 clove of minced garlic
- 1 tsp of kosher salt and fresh pepper

1. In a bowl, add zucchini (moisture removed with a paper towel), ground turkey, garlic, salt, onion, pepper, breadcrumbs. Mix well. with your hands make five patties. But not too thick.
2. Let the air fryer preheat to 375 F.
3. Put in an air fryer in a single layer and cook for 7 minutes or more. Until cooked through and browned.
4. Place in buns with ketchup and lettuce and enjoy.

Honey-Dijon Turkey Breast

Prep time: 5 minutes | Cook time: 30 minutes, plus 5 to 10 minutes to rest | Makes 8 slices

¼ cup honey
¼ cup olive oil
1 tablespoon Dijon mustard
1 tablespoon butter, melted
2 teaspoons minced garlic
1 teaspoon salt
½ teaspoon ground black pepper
2½ pound boneless turkey breast

1. In a small bowl, whisk well to combine the honey, olive oil, Dijon mustard, butter, garlic, salt, and pepper.
2. Place the turkey breast in the air fryer basket, and brush with the honey mixture.
3. Bake for 20 minutes.
4. Remove the turkey breast, brush it with more of the honey mixture, and bake for

an additional 10 minutes, until golden.

5. Let the turkey rest for 5 to 10 minutes before slicing and serving.

Turkey Sliders & Chive Mayonnaise

Prep time: 5 minutes | Cook Time: 20 minutes | Serves 6

For the Turkey Sliders:
- ¾ lb. turkey mince
- ¼ cup pickled jalapeno, chopped
- 1 tbsp. oyster sauce
- 1 – 2 cloves garlic, minced
- 1 tbsp. chopped fresh cilantro
- 2 tbsp. chopped scallions
- Sea salt and ground black pepper to taste

For the Chive Mayo:
- 1 cup mayonnaise
- 1 tbsp. chives
- 1 tsp. salt
- Zest of 1 lime

1. In a bowl, combine together all of the ingredients for the turkey sliders. Use your hands to shape 6 equal amounts of the mixture into slider patties.
2. Transfer the patties to the Air Fryer and fry them at 365°F for 15 minutes.
3. In the meantime, prepare the Chive Mayo by combining the rest of the ingredients.
4. Make sandwiches by placing each patty between two burger buns and serve with the mayo.

Chicken Jalfrezi

Prep time: 15 minutes | Cook time:15 minutes |Serves 4

For the Chicken
- 1 pound boneless, skinless chicken thighs, cut into 2 or 3 pieces each
- 1 medium onion, chopped
- 1 large green bell pepper, stemmed, seeded, and chopped
- 2 tablespoons olive oil
- 1 teaspoon ground turmeric
- 1 teaspoon Garam Masala (page 183)
- 1 teaspoon kosher salt
- ½ to 1 teaspoon cayenne pepper

For the Sauce
- ¼ cup tomato sauce
- 1 tablespoon water
- 1 teaspoon Garam Masala (page 183)
- ½ teaspoon kosher salt
- ½ teaspoon cayenne pepper
- Side salad, rice, or naan bread, for serving

1. For the chicken: In a large bowl, combine the chicken, onion, bell pepper, oil, turmeric, garam masala, salt, and cayenne. Stir and toss until well combined.
2. Place the chicken and vegetables in the air fryer basket. Set the air fryer to 350°F for 15 minutes, stirring and tossing halfway through the cooking time. Use a meat thermometer to ensure the chicken has reached an internal temperature of 165°F.
3. Meanwhile, for the sauce: In a small microwave-safe bowl, combine the tomato sauce, water, garam masala, salt, and cayenne. Microwave on high for 1 minute. Remove and stir. Microwave for another minute; set aside.
4. When the chicken is cooked, remove and place chicken and vegetables in a large bowl. Pour the sauce over all. Stir and toss to coat the chicken and vegetables evenly.
5. Serve with rice, naan, or a side salad.

Whole Roasted Chicken

Prep time: 15 minutes | Cook time:1 hour |Serves 6

- Olive oil
- 1 teaspoon salt
- 1 teaspoon Italian seasoning
- ½ teaspoon freshly ground black pepper
- ½ teaspoon paprika
- ½ teaspoon garlic powder
- ½ teaspoon onion powder
- 2 tablespoons olive oil
- 1 (4-pound) fryer chicken

1. Spray a fryer basket lightly with olive oil.
2. In a small bowl, mix together the salt, Italian seasoning, pepper, paprika, garlic powder, and onion powder.
3. Remove any giblets from the chicken. Pat the chicken dry very thoroughly with paper towels, including the cavity.
4. Brush the chicken all over with the olive oil and rub it with the seasoning mixture.
5. Place the chicken in the fryer basket, breast side down. Air fry for 30 minutes. Flip the chicken over and baste it with any drippings collected in the bottom drawer of the air fryer. Lightly spray the chicken with olive oil.
6. Air fry for 20 minutes. Flip the chicken over one last time and cook until a thermometer inserted into the thickest part of the thigh reaches at least 165°F and it's crispy and golden, 10 more minutes. Continue to cook, checking every 5 minutes until the chicken reaches the correct internal temperature.
7. Let the chicken rest for 10 minutes before carving.

Chicken & Pepperoni Pizza

Prep time: 3 minutes | Cook Time: 17 minutes | Serves 6

- 2 cups cooked chicken, cubed
- 20 slices pepperoni
- 1 cup sugar-free pizza sauce
- 1 cup mozzarella cheese, shredded
- ¼ cup parmesan cheese, grated

1. Place the chicken into the base of a four-cup baking dish and add the pepperoni and pizza sauce on top. Mix well so as to completely coat the meat with the sauce.
2. Add the parmesan and mozzarella on top of the chicken, then place the baking dish into your fryer.
3. Cook for 15 minutes at 375°F.
4. When everything is bubbling and melted, remove from the fryer. Serve hot.

Peppery Turkey Sandwiches

Prep time: 5 minutes | Cook Time: 25 minutes | Serves 4

- 1 cup leftover turkey, cut into bite-sized chunks
- ½ cup sour cream
- 1 tsp. hot paprika
- ¾ tsp. kosher salt
- ½ tsp. ground black pepper
- 1 heaping tbsp. fresh cilantro, chopped
- Dash of Tabasco sauce
- 4 hamburger buns

1. Combine all of the ingredients except for the hamburger buns, ensuring to coat the turkey well.
2. Place in an Air Fryer baking pan and roast for 20 minutes at 385°F.
3. Top the hamburger buns with the turkey, and serve with mustard or sour cream as desired.

Turkey Meatballs with Dried Dill

Prep time: 15 minutes | Cook time: 11 minutes | Serves 9

- 1-lb. ground turkey
- 1 tsp. chili flakes
- ¼ cup chicken stock
- 2 tbsp. dried dill
- 1 egg
- 1 tsp. salt
- 1 tsp. paprika
- 1 tbsp. coconut flour
- 2 tbsp. heavy cream
- 1 tsp. olive oil

1. Crack the egg in a bowl and whisk it with a fork. Add the ground turkey and chili flakes.
2. Sprinkle the mixture with dried dill, salt, paprika, coconut flour, and mix it up.
3. Make the meatballs from the ground turkey mixture.
4. Preheat the air fryer to 360°F. Grease the air fryer basket tray with olive oil.
5. Then put the meatballs inside. Cook the meatballs for 6 minutes (3 minutes on each side).
6. Sprinkle the meatballs with heavy cream. Cook the meatballs for 5 minutes more.
7. When the turkey meatballs are cooked – let them rest for 2-3 minutes.

Breaded Chicken Tenderloins

Prep time: 10 minutes | Cook time: 12 minutes | Serves 4

- Eight chicken tenderloins
- Olive oil: 2 tablespoons
- One egg whisked
- 1/4 cup breadcrumbs

1. Let the air fryer heat to 356F.
2. In a big bowl, add breadcrumbs and oil. Mix well until forms a crumbly mixture.
3. Dip chicken tenderloin in whisked egg and coat in breadcrumbs mixture.
4. Place the breaded chicken in the air fryer and cook for 12 minutes.

Chicken Cordon Bleu

Prep time: 15 minutes | Cook time: 13 to 15 minutes| Serves 4

- 4 chicken breast filets
- ¼ cup chopped ham
- ⅓ cup grated Swiss or Gruyère cheese
- ¼ cup flour
- Pinch salt
- Freshly ground black pepper
- ½ teaspoon dried marjoram
- 1 egg
- 1 cup panko bread crumbs
- Olive oil for misting

1. Put the chicken breast filets on a work surface and gently press them with the palm of your hand to make them a bit thinner. Don't tear the meat.
2. In a small bowl, combine the ham and cheese. Divide this mixture among the chicken filets. Wrap the chicken around the filling to enclose it, using toothpicks to hold the chicken together.
3. In a shallow bowl, mix the flour, salt, pepper, and marjoram. In another bowl, beat the egg. Spread the bread crumbs out on a plate.
4. Dip the chicken into the flour mixture, then into the egg, then into the bread crumbs to coat thoroughly.
5. Put the chicken in the air fryer basket and mist with olive oil.
6. Bake for 13 to 15 minutes or until the chicken is thoroughly cooked to 165°F. Carefully remove the toothpicks and serve.

Buffalo Chicken Taquitos

Prep time: 15 minutes | Cook time:10 minutes |Serves 6

- Olive oil
- 8 ounces fat-free cream cheese, softened
- ⅛ cup Buffalo sauce
- 2 cups shredded cooked chicken
- 12 (7-inch) low-carb flour tortillas

1. Spray a fryer basket lightly with olive oil.
2. In a large bowl, mix together the cream cheese and Buffalo sauce until well-combined. Add the chicken and stir until combined.
3. Place the tortillas on a clean workspace. Spoon 2 to 3 tablespoons of the chicken mixture in a thin line down the center of each tortilla. Roll up the tortillas.
4. Air fry until golden brown, 5 to 10 minutes.

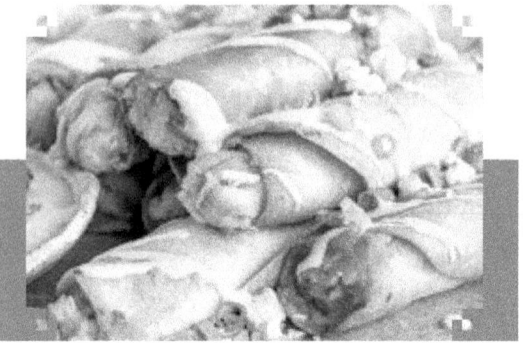

Hoisin Glazed Turkey Drumsticks

Prep time: 5 minutes | Cook Time: 40 minutes + marinating time | Serves 4

- 2 turkey drumsticks
- 2 tbsp. balsamic vinegar
- 2 tbsp. dry white wine
- 1 tbsp. extra-virgin olive oil
- 1 sprig rosemary, chopped
- Salt and ground black pepper, to taste
- 2 ½ tbsp. butter, melted
- 2 tbsp. hoisin sauce
- 1 tbsp. honey
- 1 tbsp. honey mustard

1. In a bowl, coat the turkey drumsticks with the vinegar, wine, olive oil, and rosemary. Allow to marinate for 3 hours.
2. Pre-heat the Air Fryer to 350°F.
3. Sprinkle the turkey drumsticks with salt and black pepper. Cover the surface of each drumstick with the butter.
4. Place the turkey in the fryer and cook at 350°F for 30 - 35 minutes, flipping it occasionally through the cooking time. You may have to do this in batches.
5. In the meantime, make the Hoisin glaze by combining all the glaze ingredients.
6. Pour the glaze over the turkey, and roast for another 5 minutes.
7. Allow the drumsticks to rest for about 10 minutes before carving.

Chicken Fried Spring Rolls

Prep time: 20 minutes | Cook time: 4 minutes | Serves 4

For The Spring Roll Wrappers:
- 1 egg, beaten
- 8 spring roll wrappers
- 1 tsp. cornstarch
- ½ tsp. olive oil

For The Filling:
- 1 cup chicken breast, cooked, shredded
- 1 celery stalk, sliced thinly
- 1 carrot, sliced thinly
- 1 tsp. chicken stock powder, low sodium
- ½ tsp. ginger, chopped finely
- ½ cup sliced mushrooms

1. Preheat the Air Fryer to 390°F.
2. Prepare the filling. In a bowl, combine shredded chicken, mushrooms, carrot, and celery. Add in chicken, stock powder, and ginger. Stir well. Meanwhile, mix cornstarch and egg until thick in a bowl. Set aside.
3. Spoon some filling into a spring roll wrapper. Roll and seal the ends with the egg mixture.
4. Light brush spring rolls with oil and place them in the cooking basket.
5. Cook for 4 minutes. Serve.

Ham and Cheese Stuffed Chicken Burgers

Prep time: 12 minutes| Cook time: 13 to 16 minutes| Serves 4

- ⅓ cup soft bread crumbs
- 3 tablespoons milk
- 1 egg, beaten
- ½ teaspoon dried thyme
- Pinch salt
- Freshly ground black pepper
- 1¼ pounds ground chicken
- ¼ cup finely chopped ham
- ⅓ cup grated Havarti cheese
- Olive oil for misting

1. In a medium bowl, combine the bread crumbs, milk, egg, thyme, salt, and pepper. Add the chicken and mix gently but thoroughly with clean hands.
2. Form the chicken into eight thin patties and place on waxed paper.
3. Top four of the patties with the ham and cheese. Top with remaining four patties and gently press the edges together to seal, so the ham and cheese mixture is in the middle of the burger.
4. Place the burgers in the basket and mist with olive oil. Grill for 13 to 16 minutes or until the chicken is thoroughly cooked to 165°F as measured with a meat thermometer.

Chicken Tenders with Veggies

Prep time: 10 minutes | Cook time: 18 to 20 minutes | Serves 4

- 1 pound chicken tenders
- 1 tablespoon honey
- Pinch salt
- Freshly ground black pepper
- ½ cup soft fresh bread crumbs
- ½ teaspoon dried thyme
- 1 tablespoon olive oil
- 2 carrots, sliced
- 12 small red potatoes

1. In a medium bowl, toss the chicken tenders with the honey, salt, and pepper.
2. In a shallow bowl, combine the bread crumbs, thyme, and olive oil, and mix.
3. Coat the tenders in the bread crumbs, pressing firmly onto the meat.
4. Place the carrots and potatoes in the air fryer basket and top with the chicken tenders.
5. Roast for 18 to 20 minutes or until the chicken is cooked to 165°F and the vegetables are tender, shaking the basket halfway during the cooking time.

Apricot-Glazed Turkey Tenderloin

Prep time: 20 minutes | Cook time:30 minutes |Serves 4

- Olive oil
- ¼ cup sugar-free apricot preserves
- ½ tablespoon spicy brown mustard
- 1½ pound turkey breast tenderloin
- Salt
- Freshly ground black pepper

1. Spray a fryer basket lightly with olive oil.
2. In a small bowl, combine the apricot preserves and mustard to make a paste.
3. Season the turkey with salt and pepper. Spread the apricot paste all over the turkey.
4. Place the turkey in the fryer basket and lightly spray with olive oil.
5. Air fry for 15 minutes. Flip the turkey over and lightly spray with olive oil. Air fry until the internal temperature reaches at least 170°F, an additional 10 to 15 minutes.
6. Let the turkey rest for 10 minutes before slicing and serving.

Chapter 4

Beef, Pork and Lamb

Lemon Pork Tenderloin

Prep time: 5 minutes | Cook time: 10 minutes | Serves 4

- 1 (1-pound) pork tender-loin, cut into ½-inch slices
- 1 tablespoon olive oil
- 1 tablespoon lemon juice
- 1 tablespoon honey
- ½ teaspoon grated lemon zest
- ½ teaspoon dried marjoram
- Pinch salt
- Freshly ground black pepper

1. Put the pork tenderloin slices in a medium bowl.
2. In a small bowl, combine the olive oil, lemon juice, honey, lemon zest, marjoram, salt, and pepper. Mix together.
3. Pour this marinade over the tenderloin slices and massage gently with your hand to work it into the pork.
4. Place the pork in the air fryer basket and roast for 10 minutes or until the pork registers at least 145°F using a meat thermometer.

Fried Green Beans and Bacon

Prep time: 10 minutes | Cook time:9 minutes |Serves 4

- 6 ounces Tempeh Bacon or store-bought vegan bacon
- 1 teaspoon granulated sugar
- 12 ounces fresh haricots verts (French green beans)

1. Place the bacon in the air fryer basket. Cook at 390°F for 5 minutes.
2. In an air fryer–safe pan, combine the Vegan Magic and sugar. Add the haricots verts and toss them with tongs to coat them in the Vegan Magic mixture.

3. Remove the bacon from the air fryer basket. Carefully dice the bacon. Add the bacon to the pan and toss with the haricots verts. Cook at 390°F for 4 minutes.

German Schnitzel

Prep time: 3 minutes | Cook Time: 15 minutes | Serves 4

- 4 thin beef schnitzel
- 1 tbsp. sesame seeds
- 2 tbsp. paprika
- 3 tbsp. olive oil
- 4 tbsp. flour
- 2 eggs, beaten
- 1 cup friendly bread crumbs
- Pepper and salt to taste

1. Pre-heat the Air Fryer at 350°F.
2. Sprinkle the pepper and salt on the schnitzel.
3. In a shallow dish, combine the paprika, flour, and salt
4. In a second shallow dish, mix the bread crumbs with the sesame seeds.
5. Place the beaten eggs in a bowl.
6. Coat the schnitzel in the flour mixture. Dip it into the egg before rolling it in the bread crumbs.
7. Put the coated schnitzel in the Air Fryer basket and allow to cook for 12 minutes before serving hot.

Steak Total

Prep time: 5 minutes | Cook Time: 25 minutes | Serves 4

- 2 lb. rib eye steak
- 1 tbsp. olive oil
- 1 tbsp. steak rub

1. Set the Air Fryer to 400°F and allow to warm for 4 minutes.
2. Massage the olive oil and steak rub into both sides of the steak.
3. Put the steak in the fryer's basket and cook for 14 minutes. Turn the steak over and cook on the other side for another 7 minutes.
4. Serve hot.

Easy Meatball Sandwiches

Prep time: 15 minutes | Cook time: 14 minutes | Makes 2 sandwiches

- ½ pound lean ground beef
- 1 tablespoon dried minced onion
- 2 teaspoons soy sauce
- 2 teaspoons granulated garlic
- ½ teaspoon sesame oil
- 2 tablespoons bread crumbs
- ¼ teaspoon salt
- ¼ teaspoon ground black pepper
- 2 hoagie rolls
- 2 tablespoons marinara sauce
- 2 tablespoons Parmesan cheese
- 2 teaspoons chopped fresh parsley

1. Place a parchment liner in the air fryer basket.
2. In a large bowl, combine the ground beef, dried minced onion, soy sauce, garlic, sesame oil, bread crumbs, salt, and pepper. Mix with your hands until well combined.
3. Use a tablespoon to portion out the mixture and then roll each scoop in between your hands to form a ball. This should make about 8 to 10 meatballs, depending on the size of your scoops.
4. Place the raw meatballs in the lined air fryer basket and bake for 10 minutes, flipping once halfway through, until the meat is drier and browned. The internal temperature should read 165°F.
5. Place the meatballs in the hoagie rolls, and top with the marinara sauce and Parmesan cheese.
6. One a time, return the sandwiches to the air fryer to bake, open-faced, for 2 minutes to melt the cheese and heat the sauce before serving.

Betty's Beef Roast

Prep time: 5 minutes | Cook Time: 60 minutes | Serves 6

- 2 lb. beef
- 1 tbsp. olive oil
- 1 tsp. dried rosemary
- 1 tsp. dried thyme
- ½ tsp. black pepper
- ½ tsp. oregano
- ½ tsp. garlic powder
- 1 tsp. salt
- 1 tsp. onion powder

1. Preheat the Air Fryer to 330°F.
2. In a small bowl, mix together all of the spices.
3. Coat the beef with a brushing of olive oil.
4. Massage the spice mixture into the beef.
5. Transfer the meat to the Air Fryer and cook for 30 minutes. Turn it over and cook on the other side for another 25 minutes.

Air Fryer Meatloaf

**Prep time: 10 minutes | Cook time: 45 minutes |
Serves 8**

- 4 cups ground lean beef
- 1 cup (soft and fresh) bread crumbs
- ½ cup chopped mushrooms
- cloves of minced garlic
- ½ cup shredded carrots
- ¼ cup beef broth
- ½ cup chopped onions
- two eggs beaten
- 3 tbsp. ketchup
- 1 tbsp. worcestershire sauce
- 1 tbsp. dijon mustard

For Glaze:
- half cup ketchup
- 2 tsp Dijon mustard

1. In a big bowl, add beef broth and breadcrumbs, stir well. and set it aside in a food processor, add garlic, onions, mushrooms, and carrots, and pulse on high until finely chopped.
2. In a separate bowl, add soaked breadcrumbs, Dijon mustard, Worcestershire sauce, eggs, lean ground beef, ketchup, and salt. with your hands, combine well and make it into a loaf.
3. Let the air fryer preheat to 390 F.
4. Put Meatloaf in the Air Fryer and let it cook for 45 minutes.
5. In the meantime, add Dijon mustard, ketchup, and brown sugar in a bowl and mix. Glaze this mix over Meatloaf when five minutes are left. Rest the Meatloaf for ten minutes before serving.

Pork Trinoza Wrapped In Ham

**Prep time: 8 minutes | Cook time: 9 minutes |
Serves 6**

- 6 pieces Serrano ham, thinly sliced
- 454 g. pork, halved, with butter and crushed
- 6 g. salt
- 1 g. black pepper
- 227 g. fresh spinach leaves, divided
- 4 slices Mozzarella cheese, divided
- 18 g. sun-dried tomatoes, divided
- 10 ml olive oil, divided

1. Place 3 pieces of ham on baking paper, slightly overlapping each other. Place 1 half of the pork in the ham. Repeat with the other half. Season the inside of the pork rolls with salt and pepper.
2. Place half of the spinach, cheese, and sun-dried tomatoes on top of the pork loin, leaving a 13 mm. border on all sides.
3. Roll the fillet around the filling and tie it with a kitchen cord to keep it closed.
4. Repeat the process for the other pork steak and place them in the fridge.
5. Warm in the air fryer and press START/PAUSE.
6. Brush the olive oil on each wrapped steak and place them in the preheated air fryer.
7. Select STEAK. Set the timer to 9 minutes and press START/PAUSE. Let it cool before cutting.

Vegetables & Beef Cubes

Prep time: 5 minutes | Cook Time: 20 minutes + marinating time | Serves 4

- 1 lb. top round steak, cut into cubes
- 2 tbsp. olive oil
- 1 tbsp. apple cider vinegar
- 1 tsp. fine sea salt
- ½ tsp. ground black pepper
- 1 tsp. shallot powder
- ¾ tsp. smoked cayenne pepper
- ½ tsp. garlic powder
- ¼ tsp. ground cumin
- ¼ lb. broccoli, cut into florets
- ¼ lb. mushrooms, sliced
- 1 tsp. dried basil
- 1 tsp. celery seeds

1. Massage the olive oil, vinegar, salt, black pepper, shallot powder, cayenne pepper, garlic powder, and cumin into the cubed steak, ensuring to coat each piece evenly.
2. Allow to marinate for a minimum of 3 hours.
3. When the steak is cooked through, place it in a bowl.
4. Wipe the grease from the cooking basket and pour in the vegetables. Season them with basil and celery seeds.
5. Cook at 400°F for 5 to 6 minutes. When the vegetables are hot, serve them with the steak.

Honey-BBQ Pork Chops

Prep time: 7 minutes | Cook time: 22 minutes|- Makes 2 pork chops

For the sauce
- ¼ cup ketchup
- 2 teaspoons honey
- 1 teaspoon brown sugar
- 1 teaspoon molasses
- ¼ teaspoon Worcestershire sauce
- ⅛ teaspoon ground mustard
- ⅛ teaspoon ground cayenne pepper
- ⅛ teaspoon ground cinnamon
- ⅛ teaspoon salt
- ⅛ teaspoon ground black pepper

For the pork chops
- 2 center-cut boneless pork chops, excess fat trimmed
- ¼ teaspoon salt
- ¼ teaspoon ground black pepper
- Olive oil spray

To make the sauce
1. In a small bowl, whisk to combine the ketchup, honey, brown sugar, molasses, Worcestershire sauce, ground mustard, cayenne pepper, cinnamon, salt, and pepper.
2. Refrigerate for at least 15 minutes before using.

To make the pork chops
1. Sprinkle the pork chops with salt and pepper on both sides, and place in the air fryer basket. Spray with olive oil, and bake for 20 minutes, stopping after 10 minutes to flip the pork chops and spray with more olive oil. Continue cooking for the remaining 10 minutes, or until the internal temperature reaches 145°F to 150°F and the meat is pale and mostly white with mostly clear juices.
2. Remove the air fryer basket, and brush the pork chops with the barbecue sauce. Bake for another 2 minutes to set the sauce, then serve.

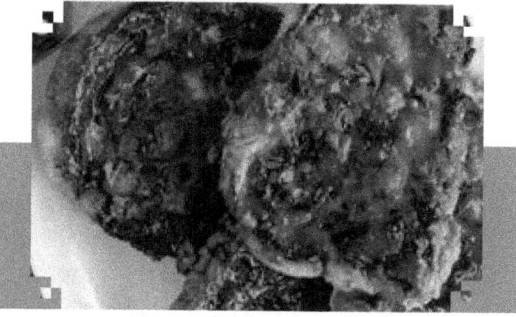

Hawaiian Hot Dogs

Prep time: 3 minutes | Cook time: 7 minutes |Makes 4 hot dogs

- 4 hot dogs
- ⅛ teaspoon paprika
- 1 tablespoon barbecue sauce
- 4 thin slices provolone cheese
- 4 Hawaiian sweet roll hot dog buns
- 2 tablespoons crushed pineapple, drained

1. Place the hot dogs in the air fryer basket. Sprinkle with the paprika, and bake for 6 minutes, until the skin looks wrinkled and slightly charred.
2. Brush the cooked hot dogs with the barbecue sauce, and bake for 1 more minute.
3. Place 1 slice of cheese in each hot dog bun, followed by the cooked hot dogs.
4. Top with the crushed pineapple before serving.

French Onion Beef Sliders

Prep time: 7 minutes | Cook time: 7 minutes|- Makes 6 sliders

- 6 Hawaiian sweet rolls
- ½ pound sliced deli roast beef
- ½ cup fried onions (like French›s brand)
- 4 thin slices provolone cheese
- 2 tablespoons butter, melted
- ¼ teaspoon onion powder
- ¼ teaspoon granulated garlic
- ⅛ teaspoon poppy seeds

1. Place a parchment liner in the air fryer basket.
2. Cut the sweet rolls in half to create slider buns, and place 6 halves in the air fryer basket on the liner.
3. Top the buns with the roast beef slices, then the fried onions, and then the cheese. Do not add the tops of the rolls

to the sliders yet.
4. Bake without the top halves of the rolls for 5 minutes, or until the cheese is melted.
5. Place the top halves of the rolls on the melted cheese, and brush the tops of the rolls with the melted butter.
6. Sprinkle with the onion powder, granulated garlic, and poppy seeds, and bake for another 2 minutes. Serve immediately.

Beef and Ale Casserole

Prep time: 10 minutes | Cook time: 1 hour | Serves 4

- Three tablespoons plain flour
- 1 ½ lbs. of leg of beef or diced braising steak
- Three tablespoons of olive oil
- Two medium onions, cut into big wedges
- 13 oz of carrots, cut into big chunks
- 7 oz parsnip, cut into large chunks
- 2 cups of strong ale
- Three tablespoons fresh thyme
- One bay leaf

1. Heat the oven to 340 ° F.
2. Spread the flour on a dinner plate. Add beef in the flour.
3. Pour two tsp of oil into a big frying pan. Fry beef on medium heat for 2-3 minutes. Fry until each side is brown all over. Shift the meat onto a plate and set aside.
4. Continue following the above instructions with the remaining meat. You can add more oil if required.
5. Put the remaining oil in a frying pan. Heat it moderately and sauté the onions, carrots, and parsnips for five minutes.
6. Then put the beef and vegetables into an ovenproof casserole dish. Pour in the ale, sprinkle the thyme and bay leaf. Cover with a lid. Cook in the oven for an hour. Wait till it is properly cooked. Serve immediately.

Sweet-and-Sour Polish Sausage

Prep time: 10 minutes |Cook time: 10 to 15 minutes| Serves 4

- ¾ pound Polish sausage
- 1 red bell pepper, cut into 1-inch strips
- ½ cup minced onion
- 3 tablespoons brown sugar
- ⅓ cup ketchup
- 2 tablespoons mustard
- 2 tablespoons apple cider vinegar
- ½ cup chicken broth

1. Cut the sausage into 1½-inch pieces and put into a 6-inch metal bowl. Add the pepper and minced onion.
2. In a small bowl, combine the brown sugar, ketchup, mustard, apple cider vinegar, and chicken broth, and mix well. Pour into the bowl.
3. Roast for 10 to 15 minutes or until the sausage is hot, the vegetables tender, and the sauce bubbling and slightly thickened.

Jamaican Pork with Jerk

Prep time: 10 minutes | Cook time: 20 minutes | Serves 4

- Pork, cut into three-inch pieces
- Jerk paste: ¼ cup

1. Rub jerk paste all over the pork pieces. Let it marinate for four hours in the refrigerator.
2. Let the air fryer preheat to 390°F. spray with olive oil.
3. Before putting in the air fryer, let the meat sit for 20 minutes at room temperature.
4. Cook for 20 minutes at 390°F in the air fryer, flip halfway through.
5. Take out from the air fryer and let it rest

for ten minutes before slicing. Serve with microgreens.

Greek Lamb Burgers

Prep time: 8 minutes | Cook time: 18 minutes | Makes 2 burgers

For the Moroccan spice mix
- ½ teaspoon ground ginger
- ½ teaspoon ground coriander
- ¼ teaspoon ground white pepper
- ¼ teaspoon ground cinnamon
- ⅛ teaspoon ground allspice
- ⅛ teaspoon ground turmeric

For the dip
- 1 teaspoon Moroccan spice mix
- 3 tablespoons Greek yogurt
- ½ teaspoon dried oregano
- For the lamb burgers
- ½ pound ground lamb
- ¼ teaspoon ground black pepper
- 2 hamburger buns
- ¼ cucumber, thinly sliced
- ¼ cup sprouts of choice

1. In a large bowl, combine the lamb, garlic paste, Moroccan spice mix, salt, and pepper, and mix together with your hands.
2. Form 2 patties, and place in the air fryer basket. Bake for 18 minutes, until the meat is drier and browned.
3. Once cooked, assemble the burgers with the buns, cucumber slices, sprouts, and a dollop of the dip, and serve.

Beef & Kale Omelet

Prep time: 5 minutes | Cook Time: 20 minutes | Serves 4

- Cooking spray
- ½ lb. leftover beef, coarsely chopped
- 2 garlic cloves, pressed
- 1 cup kale, torn into pieces and wilted
- 1 tomato, chopped
- ¼ tsp. sugar
- 4 eggs, beaten
- 4 tbsp. heavy cream
- ½ tsp. turmeric powder
- Salt and ground black pepper to taste
- 1/8 tsp. ground allspice

1. Grease four ramekins with cooking spray.
2. Place equal amounts of each of the ingredients into each ramekin and mix well.
3. Air-fry at 360°F for 16 minutes, or longer if necessary. Serve immediately.

Garlic Putter Pork Chops

Prep time: 20 minutes | Cook time: 15 minutes | Serves 4

- 2 tsp. parsley
- 2 tsp. grated garlic cloves
- 1 tbsp. coconut oil
- 1 tbsp. coconut butter
- 4 pork chops

1. Ensure your air fryer is preheated to 350 degrees.
2. Mix butter, coconut oil, and all seasoning together. Then rub seasoning mixture over all sides of pork chops. Place in foil, seal, and chill for 1 hour.
3. Remove pork chops from foil and place into air fryer.
4. Cook 7 minutes on one side and 8

minutes on the other.

5. Drizzle with olive oil and serve alongside a green salad.

Rosemary Lamb Chops

Prep time: 30 minutes | Cook time: 20 minutes | Serves 2-3

- 2 tsp. oil
- ½ tsp. ground rosemary
- ½ tsp. lemon juice
- 1 lb. (454 g.) lamb chops, 1-inch thick
- Salt and pepper to taste
- Cooking spray

1. Mix the oil, rosemary, and lemon juice and rub them into all sides of the lamb chops. Season to taste with salt and pepper.
2. Cover lamb chops and allow them to rest in the fridge for 15 to 20 minutes.
3. Spray air fryer basket with cooking spray and place lamb chops in it.
4. Air fry at 360°F for 20 minutes.

Bacon Wrapped Pork Tenderloin

Prep time: 10 minutes | Cook time: 20 minutes | Serves 4-6

Pork:
- 1-2 tbsp. Dijon mustard
- 3-4 strips of bacon
- 1 pork tenderloin

Apple Gravy:
- ½ - 1 tsp. Dijon mustard
- 1 tbsp. almond flour
- 2 tbsp. ghee
- 1 chopped onion
- 2-3 Granny Smith apples
- 1 C. vegetable broth

1. Spread Dijon mustard all over tenderloin and wrap meat with strips of bacon.
2. Place into air fryer and cook 10-15 minutes at 360 degrees. Use a meat thermometer to check for doneness.
3. When sauce starts to bubble, add 1 cup of sautéed apples, cooking till sauce thickens.
4. Once pork tenderloin I cook, allow to sit 5-10 minutes to rest before slicing.
5. Serve topped with apple gravy. Devour!

Crispy Mustard Pork Tenderloin

Prep time: 10 minutes | Cook time: 14 minutes| Serves 4

- 1 pound pork tenderloin, cut into 1-inch slices
- Pinch salt
- Freshly ground black pepper
- 2 tablespoons Dijon mustard
- 1 clove garlic, minced
- ½ teaspoon dried basil
- 1 cup soft bread crumbs
- 2 tablespoons olive oil

1. Slightly pound the pork slices until they are about ¾-inch thick. Sprinkle with salt and pepper on both sides.
2. Coat the pork with the Dijon mustard and sprinkle with the garlic and basil.
3. On a plate, combine the bread crumbs and olive oil and mix well. Coat the pork slices with the bread crumb mixture, patting so the crumbs adhere.
4. Place the pork in the air fryer basket, leaving a little space between each piece. Air-fry for 12 to 14 minutes or until the pork reaches at least 145°F on a meat thermometer and the coating is crisp and brown. Serve immediately.

Dijon Garlic Pork Tenderloin

Prep time: 20 minutes | Cook time: 15 minutes | Serves 6-8

- 1 C. breadcrumbs
- Pinch of cayenne pepper
- 3 crushed garlic cloves
- 2 tbsp. ground ginger
- 2 tbsp. Dijon mustard
- 2 tbsp. raw honey
- 4 tbsp. water
- 2 tsp. salt
- 1 pound pork tenderloin, sliced into 1-inch rounds

1. with pepper and salt, season all sides of tenderloin.
2. Combine cayenne pepper, garlic, ginger, mustard, honey, and water until smooth.
3. Dip pork rounds into honey mixture and then into breadcrumbs, ensuring they all get coated well.
4. Place coated pork rounds into your air fryer.
5. Cook 10 minutes at 400 degrees. Flip and then cook an additional 5 minutes until golden in color.

Chapter 5

Fish & Seafood

Homestyle Catfish Strips

Prep time: 1 hour 15 minutes | Cook time:20 minutes |Serves 4

- 1 cup buttermilk
- 5 catfish fillets, cut into 1½-inch strips
- Olive oil
- 1 cup cornmeal
- 1 tablespoon Creole, Cajun, or Old Bay seasoning

1. Pour the buttermilk into a shallow baking dish. Place the catfish in the dish and refrigerate for at least 1 hour to help remove any fishy taste.
2. Spray a fryer basket lightly with olive oil.
3. In a shallow bowl, combine cornmeal and Creole seasoning.
4. Shake any excess buttermilk off the catfish. Place each strip in the cornmeal mixture and coat completely. Press the cornmeal into the catfish gently to help it stick.
5. Place the strips in the fryer basket in a single layer. Lightly spray the catfish with olive oil. You may need to cook the catfish in more than one batch.
6. Air fry for 8 minutes. Turn the catfish strips over and lightly spray with olive oil. Cook until golden brown and crispy, 8 to 10 more minutes.

Almond Crusted Cod with Chips

Prep time: 10 minutes | Cook time: 25 minutes | Serves 4

- 2 russet potatoes, peeled, thinly sliced, rinsed, and patted dry
- 1 egg white
- 1 tablespoon freshly squeezed lemon juice
- 1/3 cup ground almonds
- 2 slices low-sodium whole-wheat bread, finely crumbled

- 1/2 teaspoon dried basil
- 4 (4-ounce / 113-g) cod fillets

1. Preheat the oven to warm.
2. Put the potato slices in the air fryer basket and air fry at 390°F aimed at 13 minutes. with tongs, turn the fries twice during cooking.
3. For the meantime, in a deep bowl, beat the egg white and lemon juice until frothy.
4. On a plate, mix the almonds, bread crumbs, and basil.
5. Single at a time, dip the fillets into the egg white mixture and then into the almond-bread crumb mixture to coat. Place the coated fillets on a wire rack to dry while the fries cook.
6. When the potatoes are done, transfer them to a baking sheet and keep warm in the oven on low heat.
7. Air fry the fish in the air fryer basket for 12 minutes, or until the fish grasps an internal temperature of at least 140°F on a meat thermometer and the coating is browned and crisp. Serve immediately with the potatoes.

Roasted Shrimp and Veggies

Prep time: 12 minutes | Cook time: 25 to 28 minutes | Makes 3 cups

For the veggies

- ½ teaspoon salt
- ½ teaspoon paprika
- ¼ teaspoon garlic powder
- ¼ teaspoon ground black pepper
- ½ medium zucchini, diced
- 1 cup broccoli florets
- ½ sweet onion, cut into large chunks
- ½ red bell pepper, cut into large chunks
- 1 small carrot, sliced thin
- 2 small red potatoes, diced
- 1 tablespoon olive oil
- 1 tablespoon white wine vinegar

For the shrimp

- ½ pound raw shrimp, peeled and deveined
- 1 tablespoon olive oil
- ¼ teaspoon salt
- ¼ teaspoon paprika
- ¼ teaspoon garlic powder
- ¼ teaspoon ground black pepper
- 1 tablespoon lemon juice

To make the veggies

1. In a small bowl, combine the salt, paprika, garlic powder, and pepper. Set aside.
2. In a large bowl, combine the zucchini, broccoli, onion, bell pepper, carrot, and red potatoes.
3. Drizzle the olive oil and white wine vinegar over the veggies, and sprinkle with the spice mixture.
4. Transfer to the air fryer basket and roast at   for 15 minutes, or until the veggies are fork tender.

To make the shrimp

5. In a large bowl, toss together the shrimp, olive oil, salt, paprika, garlic powder, and pepper.
6. Once the veggies are done roasting, transfer the shrimp mixture to the air fryer basket and roast at   for 10 to 13 minutes, or until the shrimp are browned.
7. Toss the shrimp with the roasted veggies and drizzle with the lemon juice before serving.

Lemon-Garlic Tilapia

Prep time: 10 minutes | Cook time:15 minutes |Serves 4

- 1 tablespoon lemon juice
- 1 tablespoon olive oil
- 1 teaspoon minced garlic
- ½ teaspoon chili powder
- 4 (5 to 6 ounce) tilapia fillets

1. Line a fryer basket with perforated air fryer liners.
2. In a large, shallow bowl, mix together the lemon juice, olive oil, garlic, and chili powder to make a marinade. Place the tilapia fillets in the bowl and coat evenly.
3. Place the fillets in the basket in a single layer, leaving space between each fillet. You may need to cook in more than one batch.
4. Air fry until the fish is cooked and flakes easily with a fork, 10 to 15 minutes.

Potato Fish Cake

Prep time: 10 minutes | Cook time: 15 minutes | Serves 2

- 1 ½ cups white fish, cooked
- pepper and salt to taste
- 1 ½ tablespoons of milk
- ½ cup of mashed potatoes
- 1 tablespoon butter
- 2 teaspoons gluten-free flour
- 1 teaspoon parsley
- ½ teaspoon sage

1. Add ingredients to a mixing bowl and combine well. Make round patties and place them in the fridge for 1 hour.
2. Place the patties into the air fryer at 375°F for 15-minutes.

Glazed Halibut Steak

Prep time: 5 minutes | Cook Time: 65 minutes | Serves 3

- 1 lb. halibut steak
- 2/3 cup low-sodium soy sauce
- ½ cup mirin
- 2 tbsp. lime juice
- ¼ cup sugar
- ¼ tsp. crushed red pepper flakes
- ¼ cup orange juice
- 1 garlic clove, smashed
- ¼ tsp. ginger, ground

1. Make the teriyaki glaze by mixing together all of the except for the halibut in a saucepan.
2. Bring it to a boil and lower the heat, stirring constantly until the mixture reduces by half. Remove from the heat and leave to cool.
3. Pour half of the cooled glaze into a Ziploc bag. Add in the halibut, making sure to coat it well in the sauce. Place in the refrigerator for 30 minutes.

4. Pre-heat the Air Fryer to 390°F.
5. Put the marinated halibut in the fryer and allow to cook for 10 – 12 minutes.
6. Use any the remaining glaze to lightly brush the halibut steak with.
7. Serve with white rice or shredded vegetables.

Quick Paella

Prep time: 7 minutes | Cook time: 13 to 17 minutes| Serves 4

- 1 (10-ounce) package frozen cooked rice, thawed
- 1 (6-ounce) jar artichoke hearts, drained and chopped
- ¼ cup vegetable broth
- ½ teaspoon turmeric
- ½ teaspoon dried thyme
- 1 cup frozen cooked small shrimp
- ½ cup frozen baby peas
- 1 tomato, diced

1. In a 6-by-6-by-2-inch pan, combine the rice, artichoke hearts, vegetable broth, turmeric, and thyme, and stir gently.
2. Place in the air fryer and bake for 8 to 9 minutes or until the rice is hot.
3. Remove from the air fryer and gently stir in the shrimp, peas, and tomato. Cook for 5 to 8 minutes or until the shrimp and peas are hot and the paella is bubbling.

Marinated Sardines

Prep time: 5 minutes | Cook time: 1 hr. 15 minutes | Serves 4

- ¾ lb. sardines, cleaned and rinsed
- Salt and ground black pepper, to taste
- 1 tsp. smoked cayenne pepper
- 1 tbsp. lemon juice
- 1 tbsp. soy sauce
- 2 tbsp. olive oil
- 8 medium Russet potatoes, peeled and quartered
- ½ stick melted butter
- Salt and pepper, to taste
- 1 tsp. granulated garlic

1. Dry the sardines with a paper towel.
2. Cover the sardines in the salt, black pepper, cayenne pepper, lemon juice, soy sauce, and olive oil, and leave to marinate for half an hour.
3. Air-fry the sardines at 350°F for roughly 5 minutes.
4. Raise the heat to 385°F and cook for an additional 7 - 8 minutes. Remove the sardines and plate up.
5. Wipe the cooking basket clean and pour in the potatoes, butter, salt, pepper, and garlic.
6. Roast at 390°F for 30 minutes. Serve the vegetables and the sardines together.

Cream Cheese Stuffed Jalapeños

Prep time: 12 minutes | Cook time:: 6-8 minutes | Serves 10 poppers

- 8 ounces (227 g) of cream cheese, at room temperature
- 1 cup of whole-wheat bread crumbs, divided
- 2 tablespoons of fresh parsley, minced
- 1 teaspoon of chili powder
- 10 jalapeño peppers, halved and seeded

1. In a small bowl, merge the cream cheese, 1/2 cup of bread crumbs, the parsley, and the chili powder. Whisk to combine. Stuff the cheese mixture into the jalapeños.
2. Sprinkle the tops of the stuffed jalapeños with the remaining 1/2 cup of bread crumbs.
3. Set in the Air Fryer basket and air fry at 360°F for 6 to 8 minutes. Serve warm.

Confetti Salmon Burgers

Prep time: 5 minutes | Cook time: 27 minutes |Serves 4

- 14 ounces (400 g) cooked fresh or canned salmon, flaked with a fork
- 1/4 cup (25 g) minced scallion, white and light green parts only
- 1/4 cup (37.5 g) minced red bell pepper
- 1/4 cup (30 g) minced celery
- 2 small lemons
- 1/2 teaspoon kosher salt
- 1/2 teaspoon black pepper
- 1 egg, beaten
- 1/2 cup (25 g) fresh bread crumbs
- Vegetable oil for spraying

1. In a large bowl, combine the salmon, vegetables, the zest and juice of 1 of the lemons, crab boil seasoning, salt, and pepper. Add the egg and bread crumbs and stir to combine. Form the mixture into 4 patties weighing approximately 5 ounces (140 g) each. Chill until firm, about 15 minutes.
2. Spray the salmon patties with oil on all sides and spray the air fryer basket to prevent sticking. Cook at 400°F (200°C) for 12 minutes, flipping halfway through, until the burgers are browned and cooked through. Cut the remaining lemon into 4 wedges and serve with the burgers.

Crunchy Baja Fish Tacos

Prep time: 15 minutes | Cook time: 17 minutes| Makes 6 small tacos

For the salsa
- 1 mango, peeled and diced
- ½ small jalapeño, diced
- ¼ red bell pepper, diced
- ¼ red onion, minced
- Pinch chopped fresh cilantro
- Juice of half a lime
- ¼ teaspoon salt
- ¼ teaspoon ground black pepper

For the fish
- 5 ounces Mexican beer (Corona, Dos Equis, etc.)
- 1 egg
- ¾ cup cornstarch
- ¾ cup all-purpose flour
- ½ teaspoon ground cumin
- ¼ teaspoon chili powder
- ½ pound cod, cut into large pieces
- Olive oil spray
- 6 corn or flour tortillas, at room temperature

To make the salsa
1. In a small bowl, combine the mango, jalapeño, bell pepper, red onion, cilantro, lime juice, salt, and pepper. Set aside.

To make the fish
1. Place a parchment liner in the air fryer basket.
2. In a medium bowl, whisk to combine the beer and egg. Set aside.
3. In another medium bowl, combine the cornstarch, flour, cumin, and chili powder.
4. Dip the fish into the egg mixture, followed by the dry mixture to completely coat.
5. Place the fish on the liner in the air fryer basket and fry for 17 minutes, or until golden and crispy, stopping to open the fryer basket halfway through and spray the fish with oil to help it become crunchy.
6. Once the fish is done cooking, place the pieces in the tortillas, top with the prepared mango salsa, and serve.

Garlic Salmon Patties

Prep time: 10 minutes | Cook time: 15 minutes | Serves 4

- 1 egg
- 14-ounce can of salmon, drained
- salt and pepper to taste
- 2 tablespoons mayonnaise
- ½ teaspoon garlic powder
- 4 tablespoons onion, minced
- 4 tablespoons gluten-free flour
- 4 tablespoons cornmeal

1. Add drained salmon into a bowl, and with a fork flake the salmon. Add garlic powder, mayonnaise, flour, cornmeal, onion, egg, pepper, and salt. Mix well.
2. Make round patties with mix and place them in the air fryer. Air fry at 300°F for 15-minutes.

Breadcrumbed Fish

Prep time: 5 minutes | Cook Time: 25 minutes | Serves 2 – 4

- 4 tbsp. vegetable oil
- 5 oz. friendly bread crumbs
- 1 egg
- 4 medium fish fillets

1. Pre-heat your Air Fryer to 350°F.
2. In a bowl, combine the bread crumbs and oil.
3. In a separate bowl, stir the egg with a whisk. Dredge each fish fillet in the egg before coating it in the crumbs mixture. Put them in Air Fryer basket.
4. Cook for 12 minutes and serve hot.

Smoky Salmon Dip

Prep time: 10 minutes | Cook time:7 minutes |Serves 6

- 1 (6-ounce) can boneless, skinless salmon
- 8 ounces cream cheese, softened
- 1 tablespoon liquid smoke (optional)
- ⅓ cup chopped pecans
- ½ cup chopped green onions
- 1 teaspoon kosher salt (or less if the salmon contains salt)
- 1 to 2 teaspoons black pepper
- ¼ teaspoon smoked paprika, for garnish
- Cucumber and celery slices, cocktail rye bread, and/or crackers

1. In a 6 × 3-inch round heatproof pan, combine the salmon, softened cream cheese, liquid smoke (if using), pecans, ¼ cup of the green onions, and the salt and pepper. Stir until well combined.
2. Place the pan in the air fryer basket. Set the air fryer to 400°F for 7 minutes, or until the cheese melts.
3. Sprinkle with the paprika and top with the remaining ¼ cup green onions. Serve with sliced vegetables, cocktail breads, and/or crackers.

Crab Ratatouille

Prep time: 15 minutes | Cook time: 11 to 14 min-utes | Serves 4

- 1½ cups peeled, cubed eggplant
- 1 onion, chopped
- 1 red bell pepper, chopped
- 2 large tomatoes, chopped
- 1 tablespoon olive oil
- ½ teaspoon dried thyme
- ½ teaspoon dried basil
- Pinch salt
- Freshly ground black pepper
- 1½ cups cooked crabmeat, picked over

1. Combine the eggplant, onion, bell pepper, tomatoes, olive oil, thyme, and basil in a 6-inch metal bowl. Sprinkle with salt and pepper.
2. Roast for 9 minutes, then remove the bowl from the air fryer and stir.
3. Add the crabmeat and roast for 2 to 5 minutes or until the ratatouille is bubbling and the vegetables are tender. Serve immediately.

Spicy Orange Shrimp

Prep time: 40 minutes | Cook time:15 minutes |Serves 4

- Olive oil
- ⅓ cup orange juice
- 3 teaspoons minced garlic
- 1 teaspoon Old Bay seasoning
- ¼ to ½ teaspoon cayenne pepper
- 1 pound medium shrimp, thawed, deveined, peeled, with tails off

1. Spray a fryer basket lightly with olive oil.
2. In a medium bowl, combine the orange juice, garlic, Old Bay seasoning, and cayenne pepper.
3. Dry the shrimp with paper towels to remove excess water.
4. Place the shrimp into the fryer basket. Air fry for 5 minutes. Shake the basket and lightly spray with olive oil. Cook until the shrimp are opaque and crisp, 5 to 10 more minutes.

Quick Shrimp Scampi

Prep time: 10 minutes | Cook time: 7 minutes | Serves 2

- 30 (1 pound / 454 g) uncooked large shrimp, peeled, deveined, and tails removed
- 2 teaspoons olive oil
- 1 garlic clove, thinly sliced
- Juice and zest of 1/2 lemon
- 1/8 Teaspoon kosher salt
- Pinch of red pepper flakes
- 1 tablespoon chopped fresh parsley

1. Sprig a baking pan with nonstick cooking spray, then combine the shrimp, olive oil, sliced garlic, lemon juice and zest, kosher salt, and red pepper flakes in the pan, tossing to coat. Place in the air fryer basket. Roast at 360°F for 7 minutes or until firm and bright pink.
2. Remove the fryer's shrimp, place on a serving plate, and sprinkle the parsley on top. Serve warm.

Parmesan Baked Salmon

Prep time: 10 minutes | Cook time: 11 minutes | Serves 5

- 2 lbs. fresh salmon fillet
- salt and pepper to taste
- ½ cup parmesan cheese, grated
- ¼ cup fresh parsley, chopped
- 2 garlic cloves, minced

1. Preheat the air fryer to 300°F.
2. Place the salmon with the skin side down on foil and cover with more foil. Bake the salmon in the air fryer basket for 10-minutes. Open the foil and top salmon with cheese, garlic, pepper, salt, and parsley. Return for an additional minute in the air fryer.

Cajun Lemon Salmon

Prep time: 5 minutes | Cook Time: 15 minutes | Serves 1

- 1 salmon fillet
- 1 tsp. Cajun seasoning
- ½ lemon, juiced
- ¼ tsp. sugar
- 2 lemon wedges, for serving

1. Pre-heat the Air Fryer to 350°F.
2. Combine the lemon juice and sugar.
3. Cover the salmon with the sugar mixture.
4. Coat the salmon with the Cajun seasoning.
5. Line the base of your fryer with a sheet of parchment paper.
6. Transfer the salmon to the fryer and allow to cook for 7 minutes.

Spicy Cajun Shrimp

Prep time: 7 minutes | Cook time: 10 to 13 minutes | Makes 2 cups

- ½ pound shrimp, peeled and deveined
- 1 tablespoon olive oil
- 1 teaspoon ground cayenne pepper
- ½ teaspoon Old Bay Seasoning
- ½ teaspoon paprika
- ⅛ teaspoon salt
- Juice of half a lemon

1. In a large bowl, combine the shrimp, olive oil, cayenne pepper, Old Bay Seasoning, paprika, and salt; toss to combine.
2. Transfer to the air fryer basket and roast for 10 to 13 minutes, until browned.
3. Drizzle a bit of lemon juice over the shrimp before serving.

Garlic Parmesan Roasted Shrimp

Prep time: 7 minutes | Cook time: 13 minutes | Serves 4

- 1 pound (454 g) jumbo shrimp, peeled and deveined
- 1/3 cup Parmesan cheese
- 1 tablespoon olive oil
- 1 teaspoon onion powder
- 2 teaspoons minced garlic
- 1/2 teaspoon ground black pepper
- 1/4 teaspoon dried basil

1. In a large bowl, toss to combine the shrimp, Parmesan cheese, olive oil, onion powder, garlic, pepper, and basil.
2. Transfer to the air fryer basket and roast at 350°F for 13 minutes, until the shrimp are browned, and serve.

Spanish Garlic Shrimp

Prep time: 10 minutes | Cook time:15 minutes |Serves 4

- 2 teaspoons olive oil plus more for spraying
- 2 teaspoons minced garlic
- 2 teaspoons lemon juice
- ½ to 1 teaspoon crushed red pepper
- 12 ounces medium cooked shrimp, thawed, and deveined, with tails on

1. Spray a fryer basket lightly with olive oil.
2. In a medium bowl, mix together the garlic, lemon juice, 2 teaspoons of olive oil, and crushed red pepper to make a marinade.
3. Add the shrimp and toss to coat in the marinade. Cover with plastic wrap and place the bowl in the refrigerator for 30 minutes.
4. Place the shrimp in the fryer basket. Air fry for 5 minutes. Shake the basket and cook until the shrimp are cooked

through and nicely browned, an additional 5 to 10 minutes.

Quick Tuna Patty Sliders

Prep time: 15 minutes | Cook time:15 minutes |Serves 4

- Olive oil
- 3 (5-ounce) cans tuna, packed in water
- ⅔ cup whole-wheat panko bread crumbs
- ⅓ cup shredded Parmesan cheese
- 1 tablespoon sriracha
- ¾ teaspoon black pepper
- 10 whole-wheat slider buns

1. Spray a fryer basket lightly with olive oil.
2. In a medium bowl combine the tuna, bread crumbs, Parmesan cheese, sriracha, and black pepper and stir to combine.
3. Form the mixture into 10 patties.
4. Place the patties in the fryer basket in a single layer. Spray the patties lightly with olive oil. You may need to cook them in batches.
5. Air fry for 6 to 8 minutes. Turn the patties over and lightly spray with olive oil. Cook until golden brown and crisp, another 4 to 7 more minutes.

Chapter 6

Side Dishes and Snacks

Szekely Goulash Pastry Bites

Prep time: 10 minutes | Cook time:19 minutes |Serves 4

- 2 teaspoons extra-virgin olive oil or canola oil
- 4 ounces Baked Chick'n-Style Seitan or store-bought seitan, cut into 1/4-inch cubes
- 1/2 cup finely chopped onion
- 1 clove garlic, minced
- 1/4 to 1/2 teaspoon salt, to taste
- 1/4 teaspoon ground black pepper, or more to taste
- 1/2 teaspoon ground cumin
- 2 teaspoons paprika, divided
- 8 ounces sauerkraut, drained well
- 1/2 cup nondairy sour cream, divided
- Unbleached all-purpose flour, as needed
- 8 uncooked vegan crescent rolls

1. In a medium saucepan, heat the oil over medium heat. Once the oil is hot, add the seitan, stirring to coat it in the oil. Add the onion, garlic, salt, pepper, cumin, and 1 1/2 teaspoons of the paprika. Sauté for 3 to 5 minutes, until the onion is translucent.
2. Add the sauerkraut and stir gently to incorporate. Cook for 5 minutes longer. Add 1/4 cup of the sour cream, stirring well, and cook for 3 to 5 minutes. Preheat the air fryer to 360°F for 4 minutes.
3. Sprinkle a work surface with flour. Place a crescent roll triangle on the prepared surface and shape the dough into a square. Roll the dough with a floured rolling pin to achieve a thin, 4-inch square.
4. Spoon 1/4 cup goulash into the middle of the pastry square. Fold by bringing each corner to the center and pinch them together to form a tuft on top.

Repeat this process to form 8 pastry bites.

5. Transfer the pastry bites to the air fryer basket. Cook at 360°F for 5 minutes, until golden brown.
6. Add the remaining 1/4 cup sour cream to a dipping bowl. Sprinkle with the remaining 1/2 teaspoon paprika.
7. Using tongs, remove the pastry bites from the air basket gently, as there may be some sticking, and place them on a plate. Serve the bites with the sour cream (and a fork and knife).

Cheese Burger Patties

Prep time: 5 minutes | Cook time 15 minutes | Serves 6

- 1 lb. ground beef
- 6 cheddar cheese slices
- pepper and salt to taste

1. Preheat your air fryer to 390°F. Season beef with salt and pepper. Make six round shaped patties from the mixture and place them into air fryer basket. Air fry the patties for 10-minutes.
2. Open the air fryer basket and place cheese slices on top of patties and place into air fryer with an additional cook time of 1-minute.

Roasted Potato Salad

Prep time: 5 minutes | Cook time: 25 minutes | Serves 4 to 6

- 2 pounds tiny red or creamer potatoes, cut in half
- 1 tablespoon plus ⅓ cup olive oil
- Pinch salt
- Freshly ground black pepper
- 1 red bell pepper, chopped
- 2 green onions, chopped
- ⅓ cup lemon juice
- 3 tablespoons Dijon or yellow mustard

1. Place the potatoes in the air fryer basket and drizzle with 1 tablespoon of the olive oil. Sprinkle with salt and pepper.
2. Roast for 25 minutes, shaking twice during cooking time, until the potatoes are tender and light golden brown.
3. Meanwhile, place the bell pepper and green onions in a large bowl.
4. In a small bowl, combine the remaining ⅓ cup of olive oil, the lemon juice, and mustard, and mix well with a whisk.
5. When the potatoes are cooked, add them to the bowl with the bell peppers and top with the dressing. Toss gently to coat.
6. Let cool for 20 minutes. Stir gently again and serve or refrigerate and serve later.

Air Fryer Egg Cups

Prep time: 10 minutes | Cook time: 10 minutes | Serves 4

- Toasted bread: 4 slices (whole-wheat)
- Cooking spray, nonstick
- Large eggs: 4
- Margarine: 1 and a half tbsp. (trans-fat free)
- Ham: 1 slice
- Salt: 1/8 tsp
- Black pepper: 1/8 tsp

1. Let the air fryer Preheat to 375°F, with the air fryer basket.
2. Take four ramekins, spray with cooking spray. Trim off the crusts from bread, add margarine to one side.
3. Add one egg to the ramekins. Add salt and pepper.
4. Put the custard cups in the air fryer. Air fry at 375 F for 10 minutes.

Rosemary Cornbread

Prep time: 5 minutes | Cook Time: 1 hr. | Serves 6

- 1 cup cornmeal
- 1 ½ cups flour
- ½ tsp. baking soda
- ½ tsp. baking powder
- ¼ tsp. kosher salt
- 1 tsp. dried rosemary
- ¼ tsp. garlic powder
- 2 tbsp. sugar
- 2 eggs
- ¼ cup melted butter
- 1 cup buttermilk
- ½ cup corn kernels

1. In a bowl, combine all the dry ingredients. In a separate bowl, mix together all the wet ingredients. Combine the two.
2. Fold in the corn kernels and stir vigorously.
3. Pour the batter into a lightly greased round loaf pan that is lightly greased.
4. Cook for 1 hour at 380°F.

Soy Curl Fries

Prep time: 5 minutes | Cook time:8 minutes |Serves 2

- 1 cup dry Soy Curls
- 1 cup hot vegan chicken broth
- 1/2 teaspoon chili powder
- 1 teaspoon brown rice flour
- 1 teaspoon cornstarch

1. 1 teaspoon chipotle avocado oil (or plain avocado oil plus 1/2 teaspoon chipotle powder)
2. Rehydrate the Soy Curls in the hot broth for 10 minutes. Drain the Soy Curls and gently press them with tongs to remove the excess liquid.
3. Transfer the drained Soy Curls to a large bowl. Add the chili powder, flour, cornstarch, and oil. Toss until well coated.
4. Transfer the Soy Curls to the air fryer and cook at 390°F for 8 minutes, shaking halfway through the cooking time.

Macaroni Cheese Toast

Prep time: 5 minutes | Cook time 15 minutes | Serves 2

- 1 egg, beaten
- 4 tablespoons cheddar cheese, grated
- salt and pepper to taste
- ½ cup macaroni and cheese
- 4 bread slices

1. Spread the cheese and macaroni and cheese over the two bread slices. Place the other bread slices on top of cheese and cut diagonally.
2. In a bowl, beat egg and season with salt and pepper. Brush the egg mixture onto the bread. Place the bread into air fryer and cook at 300°Fahrenehit for 5-minutes.

Cheesy Bell Pepper Eggs

Prep time: 10 minutes | Cook time: 15 minutes | Serves 4

- 4 medium green bell peppers
- 3 ounces cooked ham, chopped
- 1/4 medium onion, peeled and chopped
- 8 large eggs
- 1 cup mild Cheddar cheese

1. Cut each bell pepper from its tops. Pick the seeds with a small knife and the white membranes. Place onion and ham into each pepper.
2. Break two eggs into each chili pepper. Cover with 1/4 cup of peppered cheese. Put the basket into the air fryer.
3. Set the temperature to 390 ° F and change the timer for 15 minutes.
4. Peppers will be tender when fully fried, and the eggs will be solid. Serve hot.

Sautéed Green Beans

Prep time: 3 minutes | Cook Time: 12 minutes | Serves 4

- ¾ lb. green beans, cleaned
- 1 tbsp. balsamic vinegar
- ¼ tsp. kosher salt
- ½ tsp. mixed peppercorns, freshly cracked
- 1 tbsp. butter
- Sesame seeds to serve

1. Pre-heat your Air Fryer at 390°F.
2. Combine the green beans with the rest of the ingredients, except for the sesame seeds. Transfer to the fryer and cook for 10 minutes.
3. In the meantime, heat the sesame seeds in a small skillet to toast all over, stirring constantly to prevent burning.
4. Serve the green beans accompanied by the toasted sesame seeds.

Seasoned French Fries

Prep time: 5 minutes | Cook time:23 minutes |Serves 2 to 4

- 2 large russet potatoes, scrubbed
- 1 tablespoon avocado oil or extra-virgin olive oil
- 1 teaspoon dried dill
- 1 teaspoon dried chives
- 1 teaspoon dried parsley
- 1 teaspoon cayenne pepper
- 2 tablespoons chickpea, soy, buckwheat, or millet flour

1. Cut the potatoes into 1/4-inch slices, then cut the slices into 1/4-inch strips. Transfer the fries to a large bowl and cover them in 3 to 4 cups water. Soak the fries for 20 minutes. Drain, rinse, and pat dry.
2. Return the potatoes to the bowl. Add the avocado oil, dill, chives, parsley, cayenne, and flour. Toss until well coated.
3. Preheat the air fryer to 390°F for 3 minutes. Transfer the coated potatoes to the air fryer basket. Cook for 20 minutes, shaking halfway through the cooking time.

Zucchini Parmesan Chips

Prep time: 20 minutes | Cook time: 15 minutes | Serves 10

- ½ tsp. paprika
- ½ C. grated parmesan cheese
- ½ C. Italian breadcrumbs
- 1 lightly beaten egg
- 2 thinly sliced zucchinis

1. Use a very sharp knife or mandolin slicer to slice zucchini as thinly as you can. Pat off extra moisture.
2. Beat egg with a pinch of pepper and salt and a bit of water.
3. Combine paprika, cheese, and breadcrumbs in a bowl.
4. Dip slices of zucchini into the egg mixture and then into breadcrumb mixture. Press gently to coat.
5. with olive oil cooking spray, mist coated zucchini slices. Place into your air fryer in a single layer.
6. Cook 8 minutes at 350 degrees.
7. Sprinkle with salt and serve with salsa.

Air-Fried Spinach Frittata

Prep time: 5 minutes | Cook time: 10 minutes | Serves 4

- 1/3 cup of packed spinach
- One small chopped red onion
- Shredded mozzarella cheese
- Three eggs
- Salt, pepper
- Olive oil

1. Let the air fryer preheat to 375°F.
2. In a skillet over a medium flame, add oil and onion, and cook until translucent. Add spinach and sauté until half cooked.
3. Beat eggs and season with salt and pepper—mix spinach mixture in it.
4. Cook in the air fryer for 8 minutes.

Eggplant Fries

**Prep time: 5 minutes | Cook time 15 minutes |
Serves 4**

- 1 eggplant, cut into 3-inch pieces
- ¼ cup of water
- 1 tablespoon of olive oil
- 4 tablespoons cornstarch
- sea salt to taste

1. Preheat your air fryer to 390°F. In a bowl, combine eggplant, water, oil, and cornstarch.
2. Place the eggplant fries in air fryer basket, and air fry them for 20-minutes. Serve warm and enjoy!

Air Fryer Lemon-Garlic Tofu

**Prep time: 20 minutes | Cook time: 15 minutes |
Serves 2**

- Cooked quinoa 2 cups
- Lemons: two zest and juice
- Tofu: one block - pressed and sliced into half pieces
- Garlic – minced: 2 cloves

1. Add the tofu into a deep dish.
2. In another small bowl, add the lemon zest, lemon juice, garlic, salt, and pepper.
3. Pour this marinade over tofu in the dish. Let it marinate for 15 minutes.
4. Add the tofu to the air fryer basket and air fry at 370°F for 15 minutes. Shake the basket after 8 minutes of cooking.
5. In a big deep bowl, add the cooked quinoa with the lemon-garlic tofu.

Horseradish Mayo & Gorgonzola Mushrooms

**Prep time: 5 minutes | Cook Time: 15 minutes |
Serves 5**

- ½ cup of bread crumbs

- 2 cloves garlic, pressed
- 2 tbsp. fresh coriander, chopped
- ⅓ tsp. kosher salt
- ½ tsp. crushed red pepper flakes
- 1 ½ tbsp. olive oil
- 20 medium-sized mushrooms, stems removed
- ½ cup Gorgonzola cheese, grated
- ¼ cup low-fat mayonnaise
- 1 tsp. prepared horseradish, well-drained
- 1 tbsp. fresh parsley, finely chopped

1. Combine the bread crumbs together with the garlic, coriander, salt, red pepper, and the olive oil.
2. Take equal-sized amounts of the bread crumb mixture and use them to stuff the mushroom caps. Add the grated Gorgonzola on top of each.
3. Put the mushrooms in the Air Fryer grill pan and transfer to the fryer.
4. In the meantime, prepare the horseradish mayo. Mix together the mayonnaise, horseradish and parsley.
5. When the mushrooms are ready, serve with the mayo.

Scalloped Potatoes

**Prep time: 5 minutes| COok time: 20 minutes |
Serves 4**

- 2 cups pre-sliced refrigerated potatoes
- 3 cloves garlic, minced
- Pinch salt
- Freshly ground black pepper
- ¾ cup heavy cream

1. Layer the potatoes, garlic, salt, and pepper in a 6-by-6-by-2-inch baking pan. Slowly pour the cream over all.
2. Bake for 15 minutes, until the potatoes are golden brown on top and tender. Check their state and, if needed, bake for 5 minutes until browned.

Crispy Parmesan French Fries

Prep time: 5 minutes |Cook time: 10 minutes|
Serves 4

- 4 cups frozen thin French fries
- 2 teaspoons olive oil
- ⅓ cup grated Parmesan cheese
- ½ teaspoon dried thyme
- ½ teaspoon dried basil
- ½ teaspoon salt

1. If there is any ice on the French fries, remove it. Place the French fries in the air fryer basket and drizzle with the olive oil. Toss gently.
2. Air-fry for about 10 minutes, or until the fries are golden brown and hot, shaking the basket once during cooking time.
3. Immediately put the fries into a serving bowl and sprinkle with the Parmesan, thyme, basil, and salt. Shake to coat and serve hot.

Grilled Cheese Corn

Prep time: 5 minutes | Cook time:15 minutes |
Serves 2

- 2 whole corn on the cob, peel husks and discard silk
- 1 teaspoon olive oil
- 2 teaspoons paprika
- ½ cup feta cheese, grated

1. Rub the olive oil over corn then sprinkle with paprika and rub all over the corn. Preheat your air fryer to 300°F. Place the seasoned corn on the grill for 15-minutes.
2. Place corn on a serving dish then sprinkle with grated cheese over corn. Serve and enjoy!

Air Fryer Sweet Potato

Prep time: 5 minutes | Cook time: 8 minutes |
Serves 2

- One sweet potato
- Pinch of kosher salt and freshly ground black pepper
- 1 tsp olive oil

1. Cut the peeled sweet potato in French fries. Coat with salt, pepper, and oil.
2. Cook in the air fryer for 8 minutes, at 400 degrees. Cook potatoes in batches, in single layers.

Scallion & Ricotta Potatoes

Prep time: 5 minutes | Cook Time: 15 minutes |
Serves 4

- 4 baking potatoes
- 2 tbsp. olive oil
- ½ cup Ricotta cheese, room temperature
- 2 tbsp. scallions, chopped
- 1 heaped tbsp. fresh parsley, roughly chopped
- 1 heaped tbsp. coriander, minced
- 2 oz. Cheddar cheese, preferably freshly grated
- 1 tsp. celery seeds
- ½ tsp. salt
- ½ tsp. garlic pepper

1. Pierce the skin of the potatoes with a knife.
2. Cook in the Air Fryer basket for roughly 13 minutes at 350°F. If they are not cooked through by this time, leave for 2 – 3 minutes longer.
3. In the meantime, make the stuffing by combining all the other ingredients.
4. Cut halfway into the cooked potatoes to open them.
5. Spoon equal amounts of the stuffing into each potato and serve hot.

Fried Avocado

Prep time: 5 minutes | Cook time:12 minutes |Serves 2

- 1/4 cup unbleached all-purpose flour
- 1 Flax Egg
- 1/2 cup panko bread crumbs
- 1 teaspoon chili powder
- 1 ripe Hass avocado, pitted and peeled
- 2 to 3 spritzes canola oil or extra-virgin olive oil

1. Place the flour in a shallow dish. Place the flax egg in a second shallow dish. In a third shallow dish, combine the panko bread crumbs and chili powder.
2. Dredge each avocado half through the three coating stations: cover it in flour, dip it in the flax egg, and coat it with the panko bread crumbs.
3. Spritz the air fryer basket with the oil. Place the coated avocado halves in a single layer in the air fryer basket. Spritz the avocado halves with oil. Cook at 390°F for 12 minutes.

Beany Jackfruit Taquitos

Prep time: 10 minutes | Cook time:36 minutes |Serves 4

- 1 (14-ounce) can water-packed jackfruit, drained and rinsed
- 1 cup cooked or canned red beans, drained and rinsed
- 1/2 cup pico de gallo sauce
- 1/4 cup plus 2 tablespoons water
- 4 (6-inch) corn or whole wheat tortillas
- 2 to 4 spritzes canola oil or extra-virgin olive oil

1. In a medium saucepan or pressure cooker, combine the jackfruit, beans, pico de gallo, and water. If you are using a saucepan, heat the jackfruit mixture over medium-high heat until it begins to boil. Reduce the heat, cover the saucepan, and simmer for 20 to 25 minutes. If you are using a pressure cooker, cover the pressure cooker, bring to pressure, cook at low pressure for 3 minutes, and then use a natural release.
2. Mash the jackfruit mixture with a fork or potato masher. You're aiming to shred the jackfruit to a meaty texture. Preheat the air fryer to 370°F for 3 minutes.
3. Place a tortilla on a work surface. Spoon 1/4 cup of the jackfruit mixture onto the tortilla. Roll it up tightly, pushing any of the mixture that falls out back into the tortilla. Repeat this process to make 4 taquitos.
4. Spritz the air fryer basket with the oil. Spritz the tops of the tortillas as well. Place the rolled tortillas into the air fryer basket. Cook at 370°F for 8 minutes.

Chapter 7

Vegan & Vegetarian

Air Fried Kale Chips

Prep time: 5 minutes | Cook time: 15 minutes | Serves 4-6

- ¼ tsp. Himalayan salt
- 3 tbsp. yeast
- Avocado oil
- 1 bunch of kale

1. Rinse kale and with paper towels, dry well.
2. Tear kale leaves into large pieces. Remember they will shrink as they cook so good sized pieces are necessary.
3. Place kale pieces in a bowl and spritz with avocado oil till shiny. Sprinkle with salt and yeast.
4. with your hands, toss kale leaves well to combine.
5. Pour half of the kale mixture into air fryer. Cook 5 minutes at 350 degrees. Remove and repeat with another half of kale.

Avocado Fries

Prep time: 20 minutes | Cook time: 15 minutes | Serves 6

- 1 avocado
- ½ tsp. salt
- ½ C. panko breadcrumbs
- Bean liquid (aquafaba) from a 15-ounce can of white or garbanzo beans

1. Peel, pit, and slice up avocado.
2. Toss salt and breadcrumbs together in a bowl. Place aquafaba into another bowl.
3. Dredge slices of avocado first in aquafaba and then in panko, making sure you get an even coating.
4. Place coated avocado slices into a single layer in the air fryer.
5. Cook 5 minutes at 390 degrees, shaking at 5 minutes.
6. Serve with your favorite keto dipping sauce!

Chermoula-Roasted Beets

Prep time: 15 minutes | Cook time:25 minutes |Serves 4

For the Chermoula
- 1 cup packed fresh cilantro leaves
- ½ cup packed fresh parsley leaves
- 6 cloves garlic, peeled
- 2 teaspoons smoked paprika
- 2 teaspoons ground cumin
- 1 teaspoon ground coriander
- ½ to 1 teaspoon cayenne pepper
- Pinch crushed saffron (optional)
- ½ cup extra-virgin olive oil
- Kosher salt

For the Beets
- 3 medium beets, trimmed, peeled, and cut into 1-inch chunks
- 2 tablespoons chopped fresh cilantro
- 2 tablespoons chopped fresh parsley

For the chermoula:
1. In a food processor, combine the cilantro, parsley, garlic, paprika, cumin, coriander, and cayenne. Pulse until coarsely chopped. Add the saffron, if using, and process until combined. with the food processor running, slowly add the olive oil in a steady stream; process until the sauce is uniform. Season to taste with salt.

For the beets:
2. In a large bowl, drizzle the beets with ½ cup of the chermoula (see Note), or enough to coat. Arrange the beets in the air fryer basket. Set the air fryer to 375°F for 25 to minutes, or until the beets are tender.
3. Transfer the beets to a serving platter. Sprinkle with chopped cilantro and parsley and serve.

Baked Tomatoes with Feta & Pesto

Prep time: 10 minutes | Cook time: 14 minutes | Serves 4

Pesto:
- ½ cup fresh parsley and basil, chopped
- ½ cup parmesan cheese, grated
- pinch of salt
- 1 tablespoon olive oil
- 1 clove garlic, toasted
- 3 tablespoons pine nuts, toasted

Tomatoes & Feta:
- 2 heirloom tomatoes, cut into ½ inch slices
- 8-ounces feta cheese, cut into ½ inch slices
- 1 tablespoon olive oil
- pinch of salt
- ½ cup red onion, sliced paper-thin

1. Prepare the pesto by combining all the pesto ingredients excluding olive oil and salt into a food processor. Run the food processor on slow until thick paste forms. Season with salt to taste.
2. Toss tomatoes, feta, and red onion with the olive oil. Briefly, preheat your air fryer to 350°F. Arrange tomato mixture in food tray and cook for 14-minutes.
3. Portion the tomato mixture onto individual serving plates and top with some pesto and serve!

Parmesan & Garlic Cauliflower

Prep time: 5 minutes | Cook Time: 40 minutes | Serves 4

- 3/4 cup cauliflower florets
- 2 tbsp butter
- 1 clove garlic, sliced thinly
- 2 tbsp shredded parmesan
- 1 pinch of salt

1. Preheat your fryer to 350°F/175°C.
2. On a low heat, melt the butter with the garlic for 5-10 minutes.
3. Strain the garlic in a sieve.
4. Add the cauliflower, parmesan and salt.
5. Bake for 20 minutes or until golden.

Rainbow Vegetable Fritters

Prep time: 20 minutes | Cook time: 12 minutes | Serves 2

- 1 zucchini, grated and squeezed
- 1 cup corn kernels
- 1/2 cup canned green peas
- 4 tablespoons all-purpose flour
- 2 tablespoons fresh shallots, minced
- 1 teaspoon fresh garlic, minced
- 1 tablespoon peanut oil
- Sea salt and pepper, to taste
- 1 teaspoon cayenne pepper

1. In a mixing bowl, combine all ingredients until everything is well incorporated.
2. Shape the mixture into patties. Spritz the Air Fryer carrier with cooking spray.
3. Cook in the preheated Air Fryer at 365 degrees F for 6 minutes. Fit them over and cook for a further 6 minutes.

Personal Veggie Pizza

Prep time: 5 minutes | Cook time:48 minutes |Serves 1

- 8oz (225g) prepared pizza dough
- ½ cup marinara sauce
- 1 cup shredded vegan mozzarella-style cheese (Daiya recommended)
- 4 cups sliced veggies (peppers and onions recommended)
- chopped fresh basil

1. Set the air fryer temp to 380°F.
2. Roll out the dough into 4 equally sized rounds. Working in batches, place a round in the fryer basket. Top each round with an equal amount of sauce, cheese, veggies, and basil. Bake until the crust is crispy and the edges are golden brown, about 10 to 12 minutes.
3. Transfer the pizzas to plates and serve immediately.

Miso-Style Vegetables

Prep time: 5 minutes | Cook time:30 minutes |Serves 4

- 1 tablespoon white miso
- 2 tablespoons soy sauce
- 2 tablespoons rice vinegar
- 1 teaspoon sesame oil (optional)
- 2 cups finely chopped carrots
- 2 cups broccoli florets
- 1/2 cup finely chopped daikon radish

1. In a small bowl, combine the miso, soy sauce, vinegar, and sesame oil (if using). Mix well.
2. In a large mixing bowl, combine the carrots, broccoli, and daikon. Pour the miso mixture over the vegetables and toss with tongs to coat completely. Preheat the air fryer to 330°F for 5 minutes.

3. Transfer the vegetables to the air fryer basket and cook for 25 minutes, shaking every 5 minutes.

Crispy Sesame-Ginger Broccoli

Prep time: 10 minutes | Cook time:15 minutes |Serves 4

- 3 tablespoons toasted sesame oil
- 2 teaspoons sesame seeds
- 1 tablespoon chili-garlic sauce
- 2 teaspoons minced fresh ginger
- ½ teaspoon kosher salt
- ½ teaspoon black pepper
- 1 (16-ounce) package frozen broccoli florets (do not thaw)

1. In a large bowl, combine the sesame oil, sesame seeds, chili-garlic sauce, ginger, salt, and pepper. Stir until well combined. Add the broccoli and toss until well coated.
2. Arrange the broccoli in the air fryer basket. Set the air fryer to 325°F for 15 minutes, or until the broccoli is crisp, tender, and the edges are lightly browned, gently tossing halfway through the cooking time.

Pineapple Sticks with Yogurt Dip

Prep time: 10 minutes | Cook time: 10 minutes | Serves 2

- ¼ cup dried coconut
- ½ pineapple

Yogurt Dip:
- 1 cup vanilla yogurt
- 1 sprig of fresh mint

1. Preheat your air fryer to 390°F. Cut the pineapple into sticks. Dip pineapple sticks into the dried coconut.
2. Place the sticks covered with desiccated coconut into air fryer basket and cook for 10-minutes. Prepare the yogurt dip. Dice the mint leaves and combine with vanilla yogurt and stir. Serve pineapple sticks with yogurt dip and enjoy!

Veggie Burger & Jícama Tacos

Prep time: 15 minutes | Cook time:13 minutes |Serves 2

- 1 red onion, sliced
- 1 bell pepper (any color), sliced
- 4 premade plant-based burgers (Dr. Praeger's recommended)
- 1 large jícama, thinly sliced into rounds

For Serving
- diced avocados
- pickled jalapeños
- bell peppers (any color)
- chopped romaine or iceberg lettuce
- vegan cheese
- Tempeh & Walnut Tacos
- Buffalo Cauliflower Bites

1. Set the air fryer temp to 380°F.
2. Place the onion and pepper slices in the fryer basket and cook for 2 to 3 minutes.
3. Pause the machine to place the burgers on top of the vegetables. Restart the machine and cook until the veggies are tender and the burgers are heated through, about 8 to 10 minutes.
4. Transfer the veggies and burgers to a cutting board. Allow to cool slightly and then roughly chop. Scoop an equal amount of the mixture into 8 jícama shells. Add desired toppings before serving.

Veggies with Yogurt-Tahini Sauce

Prep time: 20 minutes | Cook time: 16 minutes | Serves 4

- 1 pound Brussels sprouts
- 1 pound button mushrooms
- 2 tablespoons olive oil
- 1/2 teaspoon white pepper
- 1/2 teaspoon dried dill weed
- 1/2 teaspoon cayenne pepper
- 1/2 teaspoon celery seeds
- 1/2 teaspoon mustard seeds
- Salt, to taste

Yogurt Tahini Sauce:
- 1 cup plain yogurt
- 2 heaping tablespoons tahini paste
- 1 tablespoon lemon juice
- 1 tablespoon extra-virgin olive oil

1. Toss the Brussels sprouts and mushrooms with olive oil and spices.
2. Preheat your Air Fryer to 380 degrees F. Add the Brussels sprouts to the cooking basket and cook for 10 minutes.
3. Add the mushrooms, turn the temperature to 390 degrees F and cook for 6 minutes more.
4. While the vegetables are cooking, make the sauce by whisking all ingredients. Serve the warm vegetables with the sauce on the side.

Hillbilly Cheese Surprise

Prep time: 5 minutes | Cook Time: 40 minutes | Serves 6

- 4 cups broccoli florets
- ¼ cup ranch dressing
- ½ cup sharp cheddar cheese, shredded
- ¼ cup heavy whipping cream
- Kosher salt and pepper to taste

1. Preheat your fryer to 375°F/190°C.
2. In a bowl, combine all of the ingredients until the broccoli is well-covered.
3. In a casserole dish, spread out the broccoli mixture.
4. Bake for 30 minutes.
5. Take out of your fryer and mix.
6. Serve!

Cumin, Chili & Squash

Prep time: 10 minutes | Cook time: 20 minutes | Serves 4

- 1 medium butternut squash
- 1 bunch coriander
- 2/3 cup greek yogurt
- ¼ cup pine nuts
- 1 tablespoon olive oil
- 1 pinch chili flakes
- 2 teaspoons cumin seeds
- salt and pepper to taste

1. Slice the squash into small chunks. Mix with the spices and oil in a baking pan. Roast the squash in your air fryer at 380°F for 20-minutes.
2. Toast the pine nuts and serve with Greek yogurt and sprinkle coriander on top.

Buffalo Cauliflower Wings

Prep time: 5 minutes | Cook time: 15 minutes | Serves 6

- 1 tablespoon of almond flour
- 1 medium head of cauliflower
- 1 ½ teaspoon of salt
- 4 tablespoons of hot sauce
- 1 tablespoon of olive oil

1. Switch on the Air Fryer, insert fryer basket, grease it with olive oil, then shut with its lid, set the fryer to 400°F, and preheat for 5 minutes.
2. Meanwhile, cut cauliflower into bite-size florets and set aside.
3. Place flour in a large bowl, whisk in salt, oil, and hot sauce until combined, add cauliflower florets and toss until combined.
4. Open the fryer, add cauliflower florets in it in a single layer, close with its lid and cook for 15 minutes until nicely golden and crispy, shaking halfway through the frying.
5. When the Air Fryer beeps, open its lid, transfer cauliflower florets onto a serving plate and keep warm.
6. Cook the remaining cauliflower florets the same way and serve.

Stuffed Spaghetti Squash

Prep time: 10 minutes | Cook time:10 minutes |Serves 1

- 1 small spaghetti squash, halved and seeds removed
- 4 tsp olive oil
- 1 tsp kosher salt
- 1 tsp freshly ground black pepper
- baby spinach
- diced tomatoes
- black or Kalamata olives
- sautéed mushrooms
- sun-dried tomatoes
- chopped pistachios
- shredded vegan mozzarella-style cheese (Daiya recommended)
- marinara sauce
- balsamic vinaigrette

1. Set the air fryer temp to 390°F.
2. Drizzle each squash half with 2 teaspoons of olive oil. Sprinkle ½ teaspoon of salt and pepper on each half.
3. Working in batches, place 1 squash half cut side up in the fryer basket and cook until tender and the edges are golden brown, about 20 minutes.
4. Transfer the halves to a platter. Add the recommended fillings or fill the squash as desired. Serve immediately.

Crispy Jalapeno Coins

Prep time: 10 minutes | Cook time: 20 minutes | Serves 8-10

- 1 egg
- 2-3 tbsp. coconut flour
- 1 sliced and seeded jalapeno
- Pinch of garlic powder
- Pinch of onion powder
- Pinch of Cajun seasoning (optional)
- Pinch of pepper and salt

1. Ensure your air fryer is preheated to 400 degrees.
2. Mix together all dry ingredients.
3. Pat jalapeno slices dry. Dip coins into egg wash and then into dry mixture. Toss to thoroughly coat.
4. Add coated jalapeno slices to air fryer in a singular layer. Spray with olive oil.
5. Cook just till crispy.

Chile-Cheese Cornbread with Corn

Prep time: 10 minutes | Cook time:15 minutes |Serves 6

- 2 large eggs
- ¼ cup whole milk
- 1 (8.5-ounce) package corn muffin mix
- 1 cup corn kernels
- ½ cup grated cheddar cheese
- 1 (4-ounce) can diced mild green chiles, undrained
- Vegetable oil spray
- Parchment paper

1. In a medium bowl, whisk together the eggs and milk. Add the muffin mix and stir until the batter is smooth. Stir in the corn, cheese, and undrained chiles.
2. Spray a 3-cup Bundt pan with vegetable oil spray. Line the pan with parchment paper. (To do this, cut a circle of parchment about 1 inch larger in diameter than the top of the pan. Fold the parchment in half and cut a hole in the middle to accommodate the center of the Bundt pan. Place the parchment in the pan; trim any excess parchment from around the top.)
3. Pour the batter into the prepared pan. Place the pan in the air fryer basket. Set the air fryer to 350°F for 15 minutes.
4. Allow the bread to rest in the closed air fryer for 10 minutes before serving.

Chapter 8

Appetizers

Roasted Veggie Soup

Prep time: 10 minutes | Cook time:7 minutes |Serves 1

- 8 small red potatoes, halved
- 2 cups chopped cauliflower
- 1 cup chopped broccoli
- 1 tbsp olive oil
- 1 tsp kosher salt
- 1 tsp freshly ground black pepper
- 3 cups low-Sodium: vegetable broth
- whole grain crackers or Crispy Garlic Chickpeas

1. Set the air fryer temp to 400°F.
2. Place the potatoes in a microwave-safe bowl and cover with water. Microwave the potatoes until tender, about 4 to 5 minutes.
3. Drain the water and place the potatoes in a large bowl. Add the cauliflower, broccoli, olive oil, salt, and pepper. Toss well to coat.
4. Place the vegetables in the fryer basket and roast until slightly tender and the edges are golden brown, about 5 to 7 minutes.
5. Transfer the vegetables to a medium saucepan on the stovetop over medium heat. Add the vegetable broth. Reduce the heat to low and bring to a simmer. Use an immersion or countertop blender to blend until smooth. Taste for seasoning and adjust as needed.
6. Transfer the soup to bowls and serve immediately with the whole grain crackers.

Puppy Poppers

Prep time: 5 minutes | Cook Time: 20 minutes | Serves 50 treats

- ½ cup unsweetened applesauce
- 1 cup peanut butter
- 2 cup oats
- 1 cup flour
- 1 tsp. baking powder

1. Combine the applesauce and peanut butter in a bowl to create a smooth consistency.
2. Pour in the oats, flour and baking powder. Continue mixing to form a soft dough.
3. Shape a half-teaspoon of dough into a ball and continue with the rest of the dough.
4. Pre-heat the Air Fryer to 350°F.
5. Grease the bottom of the basket with oil.
6. Place the poppers in the fryer and cook for 8 minutes, flipping the balls at the halfway point. You may need to cook the poppers in batches.
7. Let the poppers cool and serve immediately or keep in an airtight container for up to 2 weeks.

Pork and Cabbage Gyoza

Prep time: 10 minutes | Cook time: 25 minutes |Serves 4

- 1 small head Napa cabbage (about 1 pound [455 g])
- 2 teaspoons kosher salt
- 1 pound (455 g) ground pork
- 1/2 cup (50 g) minced scallions
- 1 tablespoon (10 g) minced garlic
- 1 teaspoon minced fresh ginger
- 1 teaspoon minced fresh chives
- 1 teaspoon granulated sugar
- 1 teaspoon soy sauce
- 48 to 50 wonton or dumpling wrappers, thawed if frozen
- 1 tablespoon (15 ml) vegetable oil
- Soy-Vinegar Dipping Sauce

1. Remove the cabbage core and slice the leaves thinly. Finely mince the slices. Place the minced cabbage in a colander set over a large bowl and sprinkle with the salt. Let the cabbage rest for at least 15 minutes while the salt draws out the excess moisture. Wrap the cabbage in a clean kitchen towel or cheesecloth and squeeze out as much liquid as possible. Place the drained cabbage in a large bowl. Combine the cabbage with the pork, scallions, garlic, ginger, chives, sugar, and soy sauce and knead with your hands to combine.

2. To fill the dumplings, set up a work station with a wooden cutting board, a bowl with the filling, a small bowl of water, the stack of dumpling wrappers (wrapped in plastic to prevent them from drying out), and a lined baking sheet. Place 1 wrapper on the cutting board. Spoon 2 teaspoons filling in the center. Moisten the edges of the wrapper with water. Pinch the sides of the wrapper together, pleating 1 side of the dumpling in the traditional manner, if desired. Place the filled dumpling on the baking sheet and cover with a clean towel. Repeat until you have used all the wrappers and filling. (Dumplings may be frozen at this point. Freeze on the sheet until firm, then pack into a gallon-size freezer bag for storage.)

3. To cook the dumplings, preheat the air fryer to 360°F (182°C). Combine the vegetable oil with 1/2 cup (120 ml) water in a small bowl. Brush the outside of 6 dumplings with the oil-water mixture and place in the air fryer basket. Sprinkle additional oil-water mixture on the basket. Cook the dumplings for 8 to 10 minutes, flipping once halfway through. Leave the dumplings in the air fryer with the power off for 2 minutes. Remove and cook as many additional dumplings as needed in the same manner. (Dumplings may be cooked from frozen in the same manner.)

4. Serve warm with Soy-Vinegar Dipping Sauce.

Cheese Croquettes with Prosciutto

Prep time: 10 minutes | Cook time: 7 minutes | Serves 6

- 1 lb. cheddar cheese
- 12 slices of prosciutto
- 1 cup pork rinds
- 4 tablespoons olive oil
- 2 eggs, beaten
- 1 cup almond flour

1. Cut your cheese into 6 equal pieces. Wrap each piece of cheese with 2 prosciutto slices.
2. Place them in the freezer for 5-minutes. Preheat your air fryer to 380°F. Dip the croquettes into the flour first, then the egg, and finally coat them with pork rinds.
3. Place them in air fryer basket and drizzle them with olive oil and cook for 7-minutes.

Corn Tortilla Chips

Prep time: 5 minutes | Cook time: 8 minutes | Serves 4

- 4 (6-inch) corn tortillas
- 1 tbsp. canola oil
- 1/4 tsp. kosher salt

1. Stack the corn tortillas, cut them in half, then slice them into thirds.
2. Spray the air fryer basket with non-stick cooking spray, brush the tortillas with canola oil and place them in the basket. Air fry at 360°F for 5 minutes.
3. Pause the fryer to shake the basket, then air fry for 3 more minutes or until golden brown and crispy.
4. Remove the chips from the fryer and place them on a plate lined with a paper towel. Sprinkle with the kosher salt on top before serving warm.

Grilled Curried Fruit

Prep time: 10 minutes| Cook time: 5 minutes | Serves 6 to 8

- 2 peaches
- 2 firm pears
- 2 plums
- 2 tablespoons melted butter
- 1 tablespoon honey
- 2 to 3 teaspoons curry powder

1. Cut the peaches in half, remove the pits, and cut each half in half again. Cut the pears in half, core them, and remove the stem. Cut each half in half again. Do the same with the plums.
2. Spread a large sheet of heavy-duty foil on your work surface. Arrange the fruit on the foil and drizzle with the butter and honey. Sprinkle with the curry powder.
3. Wrap the fruit in the foil, making sure to leave some air space in the packet.
4. Put the foil package in the basket and grill for 5 to 8 minutes, shaking the basket once during the cooking time, until the fruit is soft and tender.

Orange and Rosemary Roasted Chickpeas

Prep time: 5 minutes | Cook time: 12 minutes |Serves 4

- 4 cups cooked chickpeas or 2 cans (15 ounces, or 425 g each) chickpeas, rinsed and drained
- 2 tablespoons (30 ml) vegetable oil
- 1 teaspoon kosher salt
- 1 teaspoon cumin
- 1 teaspoon paprika
- Zest of 1 orange
- 1 tablespoon (1.7 g) chopped fresh rosemary

1. Make sure the chickpeas are completely dry prior to roasting. In a medium bowl, toss the chickpeas with oil, salt, cumin, and paprika. Preheat the air fryer to 400°F (200°C). Working in batches, spread the chickpeas in a single layer in the air fryer basket. Cook for 10 to 12 minutes until crisp, shaking once halfway through.
2. Return the warm chickpeas to the bowl and toss with the orange zest and rosemary. Allow to cool completely. They will continue to crisp as they cool. Store in an airtight container for up to 1 week.

Feta Triangles

Prep time: 5 minutes | Cook Time: 50 minutes | Serves 5

- 1 egg yolk, beaten
- 4 oz. feta cheese
- 2 tbsp. flat-leafed parsley, finely chopped
- 1 scallion, finely chopped
- 2 sheets of frozen filo pastry, defrosted
- 2 tbsp. olive oil ground black pepper to taste

1. In a bowl, combine the beaten egg yolk with the feta, parsley and scallion. Sprinkle on some pepper to taste.

2. Slice each sheet of filo dough into three strips.
3. Place a teaspoonful of the feta mixture on each strip of pastry.
4. Pinch the tip of the pastry and fold it up to enclose the filling and create a triangle. Continue folding the strip in zig-zags until the filling is wrapped in a triangle. Repeat with all of the strips of pastry.
5. Pre-heat the Air Fryer to 390°F.
6. Coat the pastry with a light coating of oil and arrange in the cooking basket.
7. Place the basket in the Air Fryer and cook for 3 minutes.
8. Lower the heat to 360°F and cook for a further 2 minutes or until a golden brown color is achieved

Parmesan French Fries

Prep time: 5 minutes | Cook time: 20 minutes | Serves 16 fries

- 2 russet potatoes, washed
- 1 tbsp. olive oil
- 1 tbsp. garlic, granulated
- 1/4 cup Parmesan cheese, grated
- 1/4 tsp. salt
- 1/4 tsp. ground black pepper
- 1 tbsp. fresh parsley, finely chopped (optional)

1. Cut the potatoes into thin wedges and place them in a bowl.
2. Drizzle the oil over the russet potatoes, and toss to coat.
3. Sprinkle with the garlic, Parmesan cheese, salt, and pepper, and toss again.
4. Place in the air fryer basket and cook at 400°F for 20 minutes, stirring halfway through to ensure even cooking. Top with the parsley, and serve warm.

Sage & Onion Stuffing

Prep time: 5 minutes | Cook time: 30 minutes | Serves 6

- 2 lb. sausage meat
- ½ onion
- ½ tsp. garlic puree
- 1 tsp. sage
- 3 tbsp. friendly bread crumbs
- Pinch of salt
- Black pepper

1. Combine all of the in a large bowl.
2. Take equal portions of the mixture, mold them into medium sized balls and put them in the Air Fryer.
3. Cook at 355°F for 15 minutes.

Crispy Cheese & Garlic Sticks

Prep time: 10 minutes | Cook time: 4 minutes | Serves 4

- 1 cup almond flour
- 1 teaspoon garlic, minced
- ¼ teaspoon chili powder
- 1 teaspoon butter
- 3 cubes of cheddar cheese grated
- 1 teaspoon baking powder

1. Mix the flour and baking powder. Add the chili powder, garlic, salt, butter and grated cheese, along with a few drops of water. Make sure to make a stiff dough. Knead the dough for a while.
2. Now, sprinkle a small amount of flour on the counter. Take a rolling pin and roll the dough. Slice the dough into any shape you want. Preheat your air fryer to 370°F. Set the time to 4-minutes and add cheese sticks to the basket. Serve with hot sauce!

Spicy Mozzarella Stick

Prep time: 10 minutes | Cook time: 5 minutes | Serves 3

- 8-ounces mozzarella cheese, cut into strips
- 2 tablespoons olive oil
- ½ teaspoon salt
- 1 cup pork rinds
- 1 egg
- 1 teaspoon garlic powder
- 1 teaspoon paprika

1. Cut the mozzarella into 6 strips. Whisk the egg along with salt, paprika, and garlic powder. Dip the mozzarella strips into egg mixture first, then into pork rinds. Arrange them on a baking platter and place in the fridge for 30-minutes.
2. Preheat your air fryer to 360°F. Drizzle olive oil into the air fryer. Arrange the mozzarella sticks in the air fryer and cook for about 5-minutes. Make sure to turn them at least twice, to ensure they will become golden on all sides.

Smoky Eggplant Tahini Dip

Prep time: 20 minutes | Cook time:15 minutes |Serves 6

- 1 large eggplant
- 2 tablespoons olive oil
- 5 cloves garlic, minced
- 2 tablespoons tahini (sesame paste)
- ½ teaspoon kosher salt
- 1 tablespoon extra-virgin olive oil
- ½ teaspoon smoked paprika
- 2 tablespoons chopped fresh parsley
- Raw vegetables and/or pita bread, for serving

1. Rub the eggplant all over with the oil and place in the air fryer basket. Set the air fryer to 400°F for 15 minutes, or until the eggplant's skin is well browned.
2. Place the eggplant in a bowl, cover with foil, and let steam for 10 minutes to finish cooking.
3. Holding the eggplant over the bowl, remove the skin and discard. Mash the eggplant along with the juices. Add the garlic, tahini, and salt and mix well.
4. Scrape the dip into a bowl. Create a well in the dip using the back of a spoon. Pour the olive oil into the well. Top with paprika and chopped parsley.
5. Serve with vegetables or pita bread.

Sweet and Smoky Candied Pecans

Prep time: 5 minutes | Cook time: 12 minutes |Serves 2

- 1 pound (455 g) pecan halves
- 2 egg whites
- 1/2 cup (115 g) brown sugar
- 1 tablespoon (7 g) cumin
- 2 teaspoons smoked paprika
- 2 teaspoons kosher salt

1. Toss the pecans with the egg whites

in a medium bowl. Add the sugar and spices and toss to coat the pecans with the seasoning.
2. Place half the pecans in the basket of the air fryer. Cook at 300°F (150°C) for 10 to 12 minutes, checking frequently and shaking the basket, until the nuts taste toasty and caramelized but not burnt.
3. Remove the basket from the air fryer and spread the pecans on a baking sheet to cool. (They will firm up and become crispy as they cool.) Repeat with the remaining pecans. Store in an airtight container until needed. Will last up to 2 weeks.

Apple Peach Cranberry Crisp

Prep time: 10 minutes| Cook time: 12 minutes| Serves 8

- 1 apple, peeled and chopped
- 2 peaches, peeled and chopped
- ⅓ cup dried cranberries
- 2 tablespoons honey
- ⅓ cup brown sugar
- ¼ cup flour
- ½ cup oatmeal
- 3 tablespoons softened butter

1. In a 6-by-6-by-2-inch pan, combine the apple, peaches, cranberries, and honey, and mix well.
2. In a medium bowl, combine the brown sugar, flour, oatmeal, and butter, and mix until crumbly. Sprinkle this mixture over the fruit in the pan.
3. Bake for 10 to 12 minutes or until the fruit is bubbly and the topping is golden brown. Serve warm.

Cream Buns with Strawberries

Prep time: 10 minutes | Cook time: 12 minutes | Serves 6

- 1.2 cups all-purpose flour
- 1/4 cup granulated sugar
- 1 teaspoon baking powder
- 1/4 teaspoon salt
- 6 tablespoons chopped cold butter
- 1 cup chopped fresh strawberries
- 1/2 cup whipping cream
- 2 large eggs
- 2 teaspoons vanilla extract
- 1 teaspoon of water

1. Sift flour, sugar, baking powder and salt in a large bowl. Put the butter with the flour with the use of a blender or your hands until the mixture resembles thick crumbs.
2. Mix the strawberries in the flour mixture. Set aside for the mixture to stand. Beat the whipping cream, 1 egg and the vanilla extract in a separate bowl.
3. Put the cream mixture in the flour mixture until they are homogeneous, and then spread the mixture to a thickness of 38 mm.
4. Use a round cookie cutter to cut the buns. Spread the buns with a combination of egg and water. Set aside
5. Preheat the air fryer, set it to 375°F.
6. Place baking paper in the preheated inner basket. Place the buns on top and cook for 12 minutes.

Fried Garlic Calamari

Prep time: 10 minutes | Cook time: 10 minutes | Serves 6

- 1 lb. calamari, cut into rings
- ¼ cup of almond flour
- 1 cup pork rinds
- 3 mashed garlic cloves
- 2 large beaten eggs

1. Coat the calamari rings with flour. Dip the calamari in the mixture of the eggs and the mashed garlic. Dip them in the pork rinds.
2. Cool the calamari rings in the fridge for 2-hours. Then, put them into your air fryer and apply oil generously. Cook for 10-minutes at 380°F. Serve with garlic mayonnaise or lemon wedges.

Onion Pakoras

Prep time: 5 minutes | Cook time:10 minutes per batch |Serves 2

- 2 medium yellow or white onions, sliced (2 cups)
- ½ cup chopped fresh cilantro
- 2 tablespoons vegetable oil
- 1 tablespoon chickpea flour
- 1 tablespoon rice flour, or 2 tablespoons chickpea flour
- 1 teaspoon ground turmeric
- 1 teaspoon cumin seeds
- 1 teaspoon kosher salt
- ½ teaspoon cayenne pepper
- Vegetable oil spray

1. In a large bowl, combine the onions, cilantro, oil, chickpea flour, rice flour, turmeric, cumin seeds, salt, and cayenne. Stir to combine. Cover and let stand for 30 minutes or up to overnight. (This allows the onions to release moisture, creating a batter.) Mix well before using.
2. Repeat with remaining batter to make 6 more pakoras, checking at 6 minutes for doneness. Serve hot.

Chapter 9

Desserts

Air Fryer Cinnamon Rolls

Prep time: 15 minutes | Cook time: 20 minutes | Serves 8

- 1 ½ tbsp. cinnamon
- ¾ C. brown sugar
- ¼ C. melted coconut oil
- 1 pound frozen bread dough, thawed

Glaze:

- ½ tsp. vanilla
- 1 ¼ C. powdered erythritol
- 2 tbsp. softened ghee
- 4 ounces softened cream cheese

1. Lay out bread dough and roll out into a rectangle. Brush melted ghee over dough and leave a 1-inch border along edges.
2. Mix cinnamon and sweetener together and then sprinkle over dough.
3. Roll dough tightly and slice into 8 pieces. Let sit 1-2 hours to rise.
4. To make the glaze, simply mix ingredients together till smooth.
5. Once rolls rise, place into air fryer and cook 5 minutes at 350 degrees.
6. Serve rolls drizzled in cream cheese glaze. Enjoy!

Blackberry Shortcake

Prep time: 20 minutes | Cook time:12 minutes |Serves 4

- 1 cup all-purpose flour
- 2 tbsp granulated sugar
- 1½ tsp baking powder
- ⅛ tsp kosher salt
- 2 tbsp coconut oil
- ¼ cup unsweetened soy milk
- 2 cups fresh blackberries
- 14oz (400g) canned coconut milk, refrigerated overnight
- 1½ tbsp powdered sugar
- 2 tsp orange zest

1. Set the air fryer temp to 320°F.
2. To make the cream, turn over the can of coconut milk and open the bottom. Drain the liquid (reserve for another use) and scoop the remaining solids (about ¾ cup) into the bowl of a stand mixer fitted with the whisk attachment. Add the powdered sugar and orange zest and whisk until fluffy, about 2 to 3 minutes. Set aside. (You'll have about ¼ cup of cream left over. Refrigerate for up to 3 days.)
3. In a large bowl, whisk together the flour, granulated sugar, baking powder, and salt. Add the coconut oil and use a pastry cutter to work the oil into the flour until distributed throughout the dry ingredients.
4. Add the soy milk and use clean hands to gently mix. Be careful not to overmix. Gently press the dough into a baking dish.
5. Place the dish in the fryer basket and bake until the edges are golden, about 12 minutes.
6. Remove the dish from the fryer basket and allow the shortcake to cool for 10 minutes.
7. Transfer the shortcake to a serving platter and cut into 4 slices. Top each slice with 2 tablespoons of cream and an equal amount of the blackberries before serving.

Coconut & Banana Cake

Prep time: 5 minutes | Cook Time: 1 hour 15 minutes | Serves 5

- 2/3 cup sugar, shaved
- 2/3 cup unsalted butter
- 3 eggs
- 1 ¼ cup flour
- 1 ripe banana, mashed
- ½ tsp. vanilla extract
- 1/8 tsp. baking soda
- Sea salt to taste

Topping
- sugar to taste, shaved
- Walnuts to taste, roughly chopped
- Bananas to taste, sliced

1. Pre-heat the Air Fryer to 360°F.
2. Mix together the flour, baking soda, and a pinch of sea salt.
3. In a separate bowl, combine the butter, vanilla extract and sugar using an electrical mixer or a blender, to achieve a fluffy consistency. Beat in the eggs one at a time.
4. Throw in half of the flour mixture and stir thoroughly. Add in the mashed banana and continue to mix. Lastly, throw in the remaining half of the flour mixture and combine until a smooth batter is formed.
5. Transfer the batter to a baking tray and top with the banana slices.
6. Scatter the chopped walnuts on top before dusting with the sugar
7. Place a sheet of foil over the tray and pierce several holes in it.
8. Put the covered tray in the Air Fryer. Cook for 48 minutes.
9. Decrease the temperature to 320°F, take off the foil, and allow to cook for an additional 10 minutes until golden brown.
10. Insert a skewer or toothpick in the center of the cake. If it comes out clean, the cake is ready.

Sugar-Free Carrot Cake

Prep time: 15 minutes | Cook time: 30 minutes | Serves 8

- All-Purpose Flour: 1 ¼ cups
- Pumpkin Pie Spice: 1 tsp
- Baking Powder: one teaspoon
- Splenda: 3/4 cup
- Carrots: 2 cups–grated
- 2 Eggs
- Baking Soda: half teaspoon
- Canola Oil: ¾ cup

1. Let the air fryer preheat to 350 F.
2. Spray the cake pan with oil spray, and add a pinch of flour over that. In a bowl, combine the flour, baking powder, pumpkin pie spice, and baking soda.
3. In another bowl, mix oil, the eggs, and Splenda. Now combine the dry to wet ingredients. Add in the grated carrots.
4. Add the cake batter to the greased cake pan. Place in the basket of the air fryer. Let it Air fry for half an hour.

Lemon Mini Pies with Coconut

Prep time: 10 minutes | Cook time: 5 minutes | Serves 8

- 1 box of lemon instant pudding filling mix (4-serving size)
- ½ teaspoon ground star anise
- 1/8 teaspoon salt
- 1 teaspoon pure vanilla extract
- 1¼ cups cream cheese, room temperature
- 1/3 cup coconut, shredded
- 18 wonton wrappers
- 1 teaspoon lemon peel, grated

1. Spray muffin pan with olive oil cooking spray. Press the wonton wrappers evenly into cups. Transfer them into your air fryer and bake for 5-minutes at 350°F.
2. When the edges are golden in color they are ready. Meanwhile, blend all remaining ingredients using blender.
3. Place the prepared cream in the fridge until ready to serve. Lastly, divide prepared cream among wrappers and keep refrigerated until ready to eat.

Pick-Your-Fruit Hand Pies

Prep time: 25 minutes | Cook time:8 minutes |Serves 2

For the Pastry
- 1½ cups all-purpose flour
- ½ teaspoon kosher salt
- ¼ cup shortening
- ¼ cup ([½ stick]) butter, cut up
- ¼ to ⅓ cup cold water

For the Pies
- All-purpose flour
- Fruit Filling (see Variations, below)
- 1 large egg
- 1 tablespoon water
- 1 teaspoon coarse sugar

1. Preheat the air fryer to 325°F.
2. For the pastry: In a medium bowl, stir together the flour and salt. Using a pastry blender, cut in the shortening and butter until the pieces are pea-size. Sprinkle 1 tablespoon cold water over part of the flour mixture. Toss with a fork. Move the moistened pastry to the side of the bowl. Repeat with remaining flour, using 1 tablespoon of the water at a time, until everything is moist. Gather the flour mixture and knead gently only as much time as it takes to come together in a ball.
3. For the pies: On a lightly floured surface, slightly flatten the pastry, then roll from the center to the edge into a 13-inch circle. Place a 6-inch round baking pan on the pastry near one edge. Using a small, sharp knife, cut out a circle of pastry around the pan. Repeat to make two circles. Discard the dough scraps.
4. Place half of the fruit filling on half of one pastry circle, leaving a ¼-inch border. Poke the top in a few places with a fork. Repeat with remaining filling and pastry.
5. In a small bowl, beat together the egg and water. Brush over the tops of the pies and sprinkle with the coarse sugar.
6. Place the pies in the air fryer basket. Set the air fryer to 325°F for 8 minutes, or until the pies are golden brown.
7. Cool the pies on a wire rack for at least 20 minutes before serving.

Angel Food Cake Churro Bites

Prep time: 10 minutes | Cook time: 10 minutes| Makes 3 cups

For the dipping sauce
- ¼ cup cream cheese, at room temperature
- 2 tablespoons confectioners' sugar
- 2 teaspoons butter, at room temperature
- 1 to 2 teaspoons milk

For the bites
- ½ store-bought angel food cake loaf
- 1 tablespoon ground cinnamon
- ¼ cup granulated sugar
- Olive oil spray

1. Cut the cake into 1½-inch cubes.
2. In a large bowl, whisk to combine the cinnamon and sugar. Set aside.
3. Place the cake cubes in the air fryer basket, and spray lightly with olive oil.
4. Fry for 5 minutes, or until golden brown.
5. Remove the cake bites from the fryer basket, and immediately toss then in the cinnamon and sugar mixture to coat.
6. Repeat with any remaining cake bites that didn't fit in the first batch.
7. Serve with the cream cheese dipping sauce on the side.

Blueberry Crisp

Prep time: 10 minutes | Cook time:17 minutes |Serves 4

- 2 cups fresh blueberries
- juice of ½ orange
- 1 tbsp maple syrup
- 2 tsp cornstarch
- 1 tbsp vegan butter (Earth Balance recommended)
- ½ cup rolled oats
- ¼ cup almond flour
- ½ tsp ground cinnamon
- 2 tbsp coconut sugar or granulated sugar

- pinch of kosher salt

1. Set the air fryer temp to 370°F.
2. In a baking dish, combine the blueberries, orange juice, maple syrup, and cornstarch. Mix well.
3. Place the dish in the fryer basket and bake until the topping is crispy and the berries are thick and bubbly, about 15 to 17 minutes.
4. Remove the dish from the fryer basket and allow the crisp to cool for at least 10 minutes before serving.

Mixed Berry Crumble

Prep time: 10 minutes, plus 5 to 10 minutes to macerate the berries | Cook time: 30 minutes | Makes 4 mini slices

- 1 cup fresh mixed berries
- 1 tablespoon granulated sugar
- 1 teaspoon cornstarch
- ⅓ cup old-fashioned oats
- ¼ cup all-purpose flour
- ¼ cup light brown sugar
- 4 tablespoons cold butter, cubed

1. Wash the berries, and pat them dry with a paper towel.
2. In a small bowl, toss the berries with the sugar and cornstarch. Let them macerate for 5 to 10 minutes.
3. In a food processor or small blender, combine the oats, flour, brown sugar, and butter cubes, and pulse until the mixture resembles crumbs.
4. Divide the macerated berries with juices between two mini pie pans, about 4 inches each.
5. Spoon the crumb mixture over the top of the berries.
6. Bake one at a time in the air fryer for 15 minutes each, until the topping is golden and the berries are bubbling, and serve.

Low Carb Peanut Butter Cookies

Prep time: 20 minutes | Cook time: 40 minutes | Serves 24 cookies

- 1 cup all-natural 100% peanut butter
- 1 whisked egg
- 1 teaspoon liquid stevia drops
- 1 cup sugar alternative

1. Mix all the ingredients into a dough and make 24 balls.
2. On a cutting board, press the dough balls with the help of a fork to form a crisscross pattern.
3. Add six cookies to the basket of air fryer in a single layer. Make sure the cookies are separated from each other. Cook in batches.
4. Let them Air Fry, for 8-10 minutes, at 325°F.
5. Take the basket out from the air fryer and let the cookies cool for one minute, then with care, take the cookies out.
6. Keep baking the rest of the cookies in batches. Let them cool completely and serve.

Almond Turnovers

Prep time: 10 minutes | Cook time: 15 minutes | Serves 8

- 3 apples, cored, peeled and diced
- 1/3 cup almonds, roughly chopped
- ½ tablespoon ground cinnamon
- ½ teaspoon vanilla extract
- ½ teaspoon star anise, ground
- 2 tablespoons truvia for baking
- 1 tablespoon cornstarch
- ½ pack phyllo pastry sheets
- ½ stick butter, melted
- 1 teaspoon orange peel, grated

1. In a pan, cook the apples, cornstarch, Truvia, vanilla and orange peel. Cook for 5-minutes or until apple filling thickens. Remove from heat and set aside.
2. Brush a piece of phyllo dough with melted butter; use a pastry brush. Cover with another sheet and brush again. Continue with two more sheets of phyllo dough. Then, cut the phyllo dough in half lengthwise.
3. Add 1 tablespoon of the apple filling at the end of the dough; scatter chopped almonds over the top. Fold to create a triangle. It is important that the apple filling is completely enclosed.
4. Continue with remaining phyllo dough. Brush with extra butter.
5. Place into the air-fryer cooking basket in a single layer. Bake at 345°F for 15-minutes; bake in batches.
6. Meanwhile, combine Truvia, star anise and cinnamon.
7. When your turnovers are done, brush them with some extra butter. Dust them with the seasoned sweetener and serve.

Bananas Foster

Prep time: 5 minutes | Cook time:7 minutes |Serves 2

- 1 tablespoon unsalted butter
- 2 teaspoons dark brown sugar
- 1 banana, peeled and halved lengthwise and then crosswise
- 2 tablespoons chopped pecans
- ⅛ teaspoon ground cinnamon
- 2 tablespoons light rum
- Vanilla ice cream, for serving

1. In a 6 × 3-inch round heatproof pan, combine the butter and brown sugar. Place the pan in the air fryer basket. Set the air fryer to 350°F for 2 minutes, or until the butter and sugar are melted. Swirl to combine.
2. Remove the pan from the air fryer and place on an unlit stovetop for safety. Add the rum to the pan, swirling to combine it with the butter mixture. Carefully light the sauce with a long-reach lighter. Spoon the flaming sauce over the banana pieces until the flames die out.
3. Serve the warm bananas and sauce over vanilla ice cream.

Fruit Pastry Pockets

Prep time: 5 minutes | Cook time:11 minutes |Serves 4

- 4 ounces vegan crescent roll dough
- 1 tablespoon unbleached all-purpose flour
- 6 ounces fresh blueberries, strawberries, or blackberries
- 1/2 teaspoon granulated sugar
- 1/4 teaspoon ground cardamom
- 1/4 teaspoon ground ginger
- 1 teaspoon powdered sugar

1. Divide the crescent roll dough into 4

equal parts. Sprinkle the flour on a work surface and roll the dough pieces out to 5 x 5-inch pieces, using more flour as needed to avoid sticking.
2. In a medium bowl, combine the blueberries, sugar, cardamom, and ginger.
3. Preheat the air fryer to 360°F for 4 minutes. Spoon about 1/3 cup of the blueberry mixture onto each piece of dough. Fold each corner toward the center. Work the edges of the dough to ensure it's sealed; it will resemble a pocket. Cook at 360°F for 6 to 7 minutes, or until golden brown.
4. Sprinkle the powdered sugar on the pastry pockets before serving.

Apple & Spinach Salad

Prep time: 10 minutes | Cook time:13minutes |Serves 4

- 2 cups cubed whole grain bread
- 2 tsp olive oil
- 8 cups baby spinach
- 1 medium Gala apple, chopped
- 15oz (420g) canned chickpeas, rinsed and drained
- ½ cup toasted walnuts
- ½ cup favorite salad dressing

1. Set the air fryer temp to 390°F.
2. Place the bread in a large bowl and drizzle with the olive oil.
3. Place the cubes in the fryer basket and cook until toasted, about 2 to 3 minutes.
4. Transfer the croutons to a platter and allow to cool slightly. In a large bowl, combine the spinach, apple, chickpeas, and walnuts. Top with the croutons and dressing. Toss well to coat.
5. Divide the salad into 4 bowls before serving.

Coconut Orange Cake

Prep time: 10 minutes | Cook time: 17 minutes | Serves 6

- ¾ cup shredded coconut
- ¼ teaspoon salt
- 1/3 teaspoon nutmeg, grated
- ½ teaspoon baking powder
- 1 ¼ cups almond flour
- 2 eggs
- 2 tablespoons truvia
- 1 stick butter
- 2 tablespoons orange jam
- 1/3 coconut milk

1. Preheat your air-fryer to 355°F. Spritz the inside of your cake pan with cooking spray. Then, beat the butter with Truvia until fluffy.
2. Then, press the batter into cake pan. Bake cake in air-fryer for 17-minutes, then transfer the cake to a cooling rack. Serve chilled.

Butter Walnut & Raisin Cookies

Prep time: 10 minutes | Cook time: 15 minutes | Serves 8

- ½ teaspoon pure almond extract
- ½ teaspoon pure vanilla extract
- 2 tablespoons rum
- ½ cup almond flour
- 1 stick butter, room temperature
- 1/3 cup corn flour
- 2 tablespoons truvia
- ¼ cup raisins
- 1/3 cup walnuts, ground

1. In a small bowl, place rum and raisins and allow to sit for 15-minutes. In a mixing dish, beat the butter with Truvia, vanilla and almond extract until light and fluffy. Then, throw in both types of flour and ground almonds. Fold in the soaked raisins.
2. Continue mixing until it forms a dough. Cover and store in the fridge for about 20-minutes. Meanwhile, preheat the air-fryer to 330°F. Roll the dough into small cookies and place them in air-fryer cake pan; gently press each cookie with a spoon. Bake cookies for 15-minutes.

Homemade Coconut Banana Treat

Prep time: 5 minutes | Cook time: 15 minutes | Serves 6

- 2 tbsp. coconut oil
- ¾ cup friendly bread crumbs
- 2 tbsp. sugar
- ½ tsp. cinnamon powder
- ¼ tsp. ground cloves
- 6 ripe bananas, peeled and halved
- ⅓ cup flour
- 1 large egg, beaten

1. Heat a skillet over a medium heat. Add in the coconut oil and the bread crumbs, and mix together for approximately 4 minutes.
2. Take the skillet off of the heat.
3. Add in the sugar, cinnamon, and cloves.
4. Cover all sides of the banana halves with the rice flour.
5. Dip each one in the beaten egg before coating them in the bread crumb mix.
6. Place the banana halves in the Air Fryer basket, taking care not to overlap them. Cook at 290°F for 10 minutes. You may need to complete this step in multiple batches.
7. Serve hot or at room temperature, topped with a sprinkling of flaked coconut if desired.

Appendix 1 Measurement Conversion Chart

Volume Equivalents (Dry)	
US STANDARD	**METRIC (APPROXIMATE)**
1/8 teaspoon	0.5 mL
1/4 teaspoon	1 mL
1/2 teaspoon	2 mL
3/4 teaspoon	4 mL
1 teaspoon	5 mL
1 tablespoon	15 mL
1/4 cup	59 mL
1/2 cup	118 mL
3/4 cup	177 mL
1 cup	235 mL
2 cups	475 mL
3 cups	700 mL
4 cups	1 L

Volume Equivalents (Liquid)		
US STANDARD	**US STANDARD (OUNCES)**	**METRIC (AP-PROXIMATE)**
2 tablespoons	1 fl.oz.	30 mL
1/4 cup	2 fl.oz.	60 mL
1/2 cup	4 fl.oz.	120 mL
1 cup	8 fl.oz.	240 mL
1 1/2 cup	12 fl.oz.	355 mL
2 cups or 1 pint	16 fl.oz.	475 mL
4 cups or 1 quart	32 fl.oz.	1 L
1 gallon	128 fl.oz.	4 L

Temperatures Equivalents	
FAHRENHEIT(F)	**CELSIUS(C) APPROXIMATE)**
225 °F	107 °C
250 °F	120 ° °C
275 °F	135 °C
300 °F	150 °C
325 °F	160 °C
350 °F	180 °C
375 °F	190 °C
400 °F	205 °C
425 °F	220 °C
450 °F	235 °C
475 °F	245 °C
500 °F	260 °C

Weight Equivalents	
US STANDARD	**METRIC (APPROXIMATE)**
1 ounce	28 g
2 ounces	57 g
5 ounces	142 g
10 ounces	284 g
15 ounces	425 g
16 ounces (1 pound)	455 g
1.5 pounds	680 g
2 pounds	907 g

Appendix 2 The Dirty Dozen and Clean Fifteen

The Environmental Working Group (EWG) is a nonprofit, nonpartisan organization dedicated to protecting human health and the environment Its mission is to empower people to live healthier lives in a healthier environment. This organization publishes an annual list of the twelve kinds of produce, in sequence, that have the highest amount of pesticide residue-the Dirty Dozen-as well as a list of the fifteen kinds ofproduce that have the least amount of pesticide residue-the Clean Fifteen.

THE DIRTY DOZEN	
The 2016 Dirty Dozen includes the following produce. These are considered among the year's most important produce to buy organic:	
Strawberries	Spinach
Apples	Tomatoes
Nectarines	Bell peppers
Peaches	Cherry tomatoes
Celery	Cucumbers
Grapes	Kale/collard greens
Cherries	Hot peppers

The Dirty Dozen list contains two additional itemskale/collard greens and hot peppers-because they tend to contain trace levels of highly hazardous pesticides.

THE CLEAN FIFTEEN	
The least critical to buy organically are the Clean Fifteen list. The following are on the 2016 list:	
Avocados	Papayas
Corn	Kiw
Pineapples	Eggplant
Cabbage	Honeydew
Sweet peas	Grapefruit
Onions	Cantaloupe
Asparagus	Cauliflower
Mangos	

Some of the sweet corn sold in the United States are made from genetically engineered (GE) seedstock. Buy organic varieties of these crops to avoid GE produce.

Appendix 3 Index

Jacqueline R. Izaguirre